S0-DNH-961

"In a moment in which 'resistance' is a hashtag and 'wholeness' is an industry, Curtice's *Living Resistance*—a reckoning, reclaiming, and remembering—is a lifeline reconnecting us with our human calling. Curtice beautifully honors the ancient and eternal promise of liberation as not only our sacred birthright but our marching orders."

—**Glennon Doyle**, #1 *New York Times* bestselling author of *Untamed*; founder of Together Rising

"*Living Resistance* forges a path to a more whole now and a more whole tomorrow. It shows how healing ourselves, our communities, our Earth, and our society are all inextricable, and how to gently integrate all levels of being and doing so that our daily acts of living become ways of resisting oppressive forces and bringing new possibilities into being."

—**Rabbi Danya Ruttenberg**, author of *On Repentance and Repair*

"For those who have been hearing the call for a more equitable, compassionate, and humane world, *Living Resistance* is the road map we have been looking for. Curtice invites us into a multi-layered understanding of resistance with love and justice at the center. Through a tapestry of ancestral, personal, and collective wisdom, she shares both practically and poetically. In a time where we are being invited to rise up and move toward liberation for all of our kin, this book reminds us of the fire we hold in our bellies and the spark we carry in our souls. I am so grateful that this book exists; it's a must-read for all."

—**Asha Frost**, Indigenous Medicine Woman; bestselling author of *You Are the Medicine*

"As a rabbi, as a Jew, and as a human, I am profoundly grateful to Curtice for inviting us into the sacred realm of Indigenous wisdom. For all of us rooted in a faith tradition that seeks healing for a broken world, this inspiring book offers an accessible path of resistance to oppression. May every reader of every background find joy in journeying toward liberation and wholeness together."

—**Rabbi Jonah Dov Pesner**, director, Religious Action Center; senior vice president, Union for Reform Judaism

LIVING RESISTANCE

Previous Books by the Author

Native: Identity, Belonging, and Rediscovering God
Glory Happening: Finding the Divine in Everyday Places

LIVING RESISTANCE

An Indigenous Vision
for Seeking Wholeness Every Day

KAITLIN B. CURTICE

Brazos Press

a division of Baker Publishing Group
Grand Rapids, Michigan

© 2023 by Kaitlin B. Curtice

Published by Brazos Press
a division of Baker Publishing Group
Grand Rapids, Michigan
www.brazospress.com

Printed in the United States of America

All rights reserved. No part of this publication may be reproduced, stored in a retrieval system, or transmitted in any form or by any means—for example, electronic, photocopy, recording—without the prior written permission of the publisher. The only exception is brief quotations in printed reviews.

Library of Congress Cataloging-in-Publication Data
Names: Curtice, Kaitlin B., author.
Title: Living resistance : an indigenous vision for seeking wholeness every day / Kaitlin B. Curtice.
Description: Grand Rapids, Michigan : Brazos Press, a division of Baker Publishing Group, [2023] | Includes bibliographical references.
Identifiers: LCCN 2022028505 | ISBN 9781587435713 (cloth) | ISBN 9781493440337 (pdf) | ISBN 9781493440320 (ebook)
Subjects: LCSH: Spirituality. | Spiritual life.
Classification: LCC BL624 .C875 2023 | DDC 204/.40897—dc23/eng20220917
LC record available at https://lccn.loc.gov/2022028505

Unless otherwise indicated, Scripture quotations are from THE HOLY BIBLE, NEW INTERNATIONAL VERSION®, NIV® Copyright © 1973, 1978, 1984, 2011 by Biblica, Inc.® Used by permission. All rights reserved worldwide.

Published in association with Gardner Literary, LLC. www.gardner-literary.com.

Cover art and interior illustrations © Alanah Astehtsi Otsistohkwa Jewell / Bear Clan, Oneida Nation.

Baker Publishing Group publications use paper produced from sustainable forestry practices and post-consumer waste whenever possible.

23   24   25   26   27   28   29   7   6   5   4   3   2   1

To Trav

One January day you wrote to me:
You are a writer.
You love God.
There are many forms of God and they all love you.
Write.

Thank you for reminding me.
Thank you for being my partner and constant.
Thank you for living resistance with me, always.

CONTENTS

Introduction   11

PART 1 THE PERSONAL REALM   19

1. What Is Resistance?   23
2. Art as Resistance   30
3. Presence as Resistance   38
4. Embodiment as Resistance   47
5. Radical Self-Love as Resistance   54

PART 2 THE COMMUNAL REALM   63

6. Childcare as Resistance   67
7. Ethical Practices as Resistance   76
8. Solidarity Work as Resistance   84
9. Protecting the Land as Resistance   93
10. Kinship as Resistance   101

PART 3 THE ANCESTRAL REALM 111

11. Decolonizing as Resistance 115

12. Generosity as Resistance 124

13. Intergenerational Healing as Resistance 132

14. Liminality as Resistance 139

15. Facing History as Resistance 147

PART 4 THE INTEGRAL REALM 155

16. Integration as Resistance 159

17. Interspiritual Relationship as Resistance 166

18. Prayer as Resistance 172

19. Dreaming as Resistance 178

20. Lifelong Resistance 185

Acknowledgments 193

Notes 195

Author Bio 203

INTRODUCTION

Were you born to resist
Or be abused?
The Foo Fighters,
"Best of You"

Dear Reader, Feeler, Explorer, Un-learner, and Friend,

I want you to remember something really important as you read this book: you are a human being. You have not yet arrived, but you are continually arriving. The thing about being human is that we are born, we live, we grieve, and we celebrate, and one day we pass on, becoming ancestors and guides to those who come after us.

One of the most painful things I notice in my work is that people are scared to start the journey of transformation because they don't know when they will be done. They think a week of reading the right books will get them there, only to find out that is not enough. They believe that following the right people on Instagram and Twitter will alleviate them of ignorance, but it doesn't. So they give up. They stop reading the books and they go back to whatever status quo they held on to, assuring *themselves that change isn't really possible or that the effort isn't worth it in such a hopeless world. <u>We forget that living is our actual adventure,</u> the flesh and blood and spirit with which we journey the Earth together into the life that waits after this one. It all matters. So take a deep breath as you read this next line:*

<u>You are a human being. You are always arriving.</u>

The timeline of your life is not a straight line, after all; it is a series of ebbs and flows, backs and forths, heres and theres. You are nowhere and everywhere all at once, and that means that most of the time, the best you can do is be present to the moment, be open to the unlearning and the learning, and trust that you're doing the work of Love.

As you read this book, you may get overwhelmed. When you do, come back to this page and read these words again. Repeat them to yourself as a kind of medicine: **I am a human being. I am always arriving.**

Now, let's get started.

Today the old one inside you is collecting bones. What is she re-making? She is the soul self, the builder of the soul-home. *Ella lo hace a mano,* she makes and re-makes the soul by hand. What is she making for you?

Clarissa Pinkola Estés, *Women Who Run with the Wolves*

Where does resistance begin, and where does it end?

Perhaps we need to stop thinking of our processes as linear and embrace them as a journey that is at best cyclical and often labyrinthine, with twists and turns, entrances and exits. Maybe resistance overlaps in the different realms of our life, realms that are real and connected to one another.

This book is titled *Living Resistance* for a number of reasons. First, resistance itself is a living, breathing being—when we enter

[handwritten margin note: irregular + twisting]

into the flow of resistance, we enter into a sacred, embodied, connected way of being that brings freedom and wholeness.

Second, living is an active, ongoing, cyclical embodiment. When we choose to live resistance, we are choosing to practice it with all that we are and all that we have. This is what it means to be human. This is how we understand stories and histories. This is how we hold space for one another and for Mother Earth.

I encourage you to mark up this book, if you're reading a print version. I hope you'll doodle in the margins, highlight and underline, ask questions. And if you're listening to the audiobook, I hope you'll keep a journal on the side or take mental notes in some other way. This book is meant to be a journey, and I've included places throughout the chapters where you can stop and process, take a breath, and answer a few questions as we go.

The subtitle of this book, *An Indigenous Vision for Seeking Wholeness Every Day*, reflects what I've already tried to convey— we are seekers, grabbing at wholeness, digging deeper, looking for magic, and asking what it all means.

This book is grounded in my own visions for a better world, both as an Indigenous woman and as someone who is constantly searching my personal world and the world outside of myself for evidence of God or the Sacred. Indigenous realities, visions, and practices all over the world have led people throughout history, just as they lead us today, toward kinship and belonging with Mother Earth and with one another. My hope is that this book tethers us to that conversation and to practices that help us understand how the world works in those cycles and seasons around and in us—awakening us to ourselves, one another, and this sacred world.

It's true that many of us are awakened out of a kind of deep sleep to our need to seek wholeness in the world. Our children get bullied at school so we fight the toxic forces of racism and patriarchy; we leave the fundamentalist upbringing we grew up in because we come to honor the integrity and humanity of our gender-nonbinary and trans friends; we attend our first Black Lives Matter protest and realize that we haven't done enough to actively fight against systems of white supremacy and to see white supremacy's legacy lived out in ourselves; we are made aware of our ableism and begin to dismantle the systems and very staircases that aren't accessible to everyone.

If you are here, reading this book, you may have had one of those moments, or maybe you're in the middle of that moment right now. So how can we embody the work of resistance on physical, spiritual, socioeconomic, mental, and political levels? How can we embody solidarity not just with one another but with all the creatures of this earth, human and otherwise, and with Mother Earth herself—with, as we call her in Potawatomi, *Segmekwe?*

This book is organized into four parts, a framework I call the "realms of resistance." They are connected but separate; they overlap to make us whole as people. These four realms are the personal, the communal, the ancestral, and the integral. As I stated earlier, this journey is not linear. So, too, the realms in which we practice and embody resistance are not linear. We can move from realm to realm, we can inhabit more than one space, and we can journey back to a realm we thought we would never again visit—it is supposed to be this way, the way of being human.

So why *realms?* Traditionally we think of a realm as either a kingdom or a geographical area. I mean something closer to the second idea. I want us to think of these four realms of resistance not so much as kingdoms but as spaces and places that we might inhabit or, in a more spiritual sense, embody. We live and exist there, always, in one realm or another, or in the overlap of many.

The realms are arranged by color, season, and other characteristics. On the cover of the book, you can see the realms of resistance in their full beauty, and I hope you'll linger with that illustration as you ask yourself how you have moved among the realms in your own life.

[handwritten margin note: this is always for/go to/her about, not just humans]

Here is a brief description of each realm:

Personal Realm: This realm's color is red, to represent our lifeblood, the connection to our *dé* (heart center). It is the season of winter, the time when we go inward to understand, ask questions, rest, and process.

Communal Realm: This realm's color is brown, to represent *aki*—dirt or earth. It is the time to honor our connection to the land and each other, and the time to plant seeds and make changes on the communal level. It is spring, the time of planting and waiting.

Ancestral Realm: This realm's color is blue, to represent *mbish* (water), fluidity, movement, and the space we inhabit as we interact with our ancestors. Resistance is fluid, moving work. It is the season of summer, when we notice what grows and blooms for future generations, what comes out of the hard work of planting that we did in the Communal Realm.

Integral Realm: This realm's color is yellow, and it is at the very center of who we are, our *shkode* (fire). In this realm, we integrate all the embodiment, presence, and work of the other realms. The Integral Realm, the season of autumn, is the time to harvest, to gather in all that we've learned, unlearned, and embodied in the other realms.

It is important that these realms reflect the gifts of Mother Earth around us. As we move between the realms in our daily lives, let's remember to honor the gifts we've been given along the way, honoring one another, ourselves, and the journey toward wholeness.

Religions and spiritual backgrounds around the world and throughout time have held core values that tethered them to Earth and to one another. As humans, we are to practice kinship, belonging, and love—we are wired for resistance, for activism, for the work of shaping spaces and movements that ask for peace and hope.

In Judaism, the values of lovingkindness, of respect for one another's humanity, and of shalom, or the pursuit of wholeness in the world, are widely held as tenets of the faith.[1] Sikhism values things like equality between men and women, community service, and diversity.[2] Humanists gather their values from love and hope in humanity itself, not by following any supernatural being but by being present to the life we have on Earth.[3] Christians hold to the value of loving neighbor as self, a command given by Jesus in the New Testament Gospel of Mark (12:31). My Potawatomi ancestors believed in the Seven Grandfather Teachings—love, respect, bravery, honesty, truth, humility, and wisdom—among other things, and we follow these teachings today to know what it means to live in a good way, to honor ourselves, our ancestors, each other, Earth, and all who come after us.[4]

These are just a few of the many ways we understand The Sacred in our lives. When we draw from the richness of others' practices, we learn more fully what it means to be human.

Our inner work is connected to our outer work, so resistance requires great care for ourselves to feel connected and whole. When we learn to care for and consider our own spiritual values, we will learn to value what others hold important as well. I value what my Sikh, Muslim, Hindu, Buddhist, Animist, Atheist, Humanist, Indigenous, Christian, and Jewish friends bring to the table because we, all of us together, have created the world we live in today. We are a product, and we are producers at the same time. If we can learn to look critically yet lovingly at our own contexts, to ask hard questions and challenge ourselves, we will learn to do the same for one another, and the Seven Grandfather Teachings will find space in our relationships and in the work we do.

Storytelling is key to this work. Storytelling flies in the face of a Western, colonized mindset that says we must get the work done *now or never*. When we slow down and engage in the work of storytelling and story sharing, something sacred happens every single time. We are more fully prepared for wherever our own journeys take us, and along the way we are considerate of one another, holding kinship at the forefront of our minds and hearts. Never underestimate the ripple effects even one relationship can have on your own world and the world outside of you.

My hope is that this book provides a space for us to examine this journey together.

I believe that at the core of the human soul we are called to be liberators and resisters. We are called to fight systems of oppression that make life harder for our human and nonhuman kin. Some of us lose our path along the way and knowingly or unknowingly uphold the status quo of empire only to meander our way back again, but there are also those who spend their entire lives doing the hard and beautiful work of wholeness-making in this world, through decolonizing and fighting against systems that oppress. This is not a shallow book on hobby resistance that requires little from us yet gives us the chance to say that we resisted something. This book is a call deeper in and also forward, toward liberation, and if we let it, this movement toward liberation will become the very rhythm of our lives.

In an era in which "activism" and "resistance" are tokenized hot topics, I want to restore these ideas as a basic human calling, one that each of us lives into every day that we fight for Love. Activism and resistance are not fads; they are lifelong embodiments, a lot like decolonization, which is about reclaiming and proclaiming belovedness alongside those who have been abandoned and dismissed by empire. No matter who you are or what you "do" in the world, you have a role to play in finding, understanding, and sharing sacredness, and your acts of extraordinary resistance are the truths that hold us all together.

In this book, we will take a journey to discover that oppression in history repeats itself, but it doesn't have to. As regular people, we can make everyday choices that are the work of liberation not

this is so very important

only for ourselves but for all our kin. And we can trust that every move we make, whether on the micro or the macro level or somewhere in between, has ripple effects that will bring nourishment to the world.

This is Living Resistance.

i love the positive language and mindset

PART 1

THE PERSONAL REALM

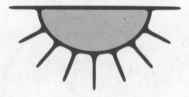

I'm my own soulmate.

LIZZO, "Soulmate"

❦ THE PERSONAL REALM ❦

is the color red, to represent our lifeblood, the connection to our *dé* (heart center). It is the season of winter, the time when we go inward to understand, ask questions, rest, and process.

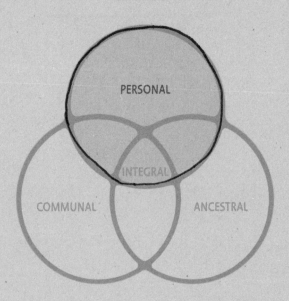

What is a poem?
It is the quietest,
softest part of you,
held to an invisible microphone,
held up to the light,
held up beyond the
hustle and bustle of the day
and the groaning aches of the night.

A poem is the anger
that releases itself
in your time of greatest need,
when you are ready to fracture
before you believe again,
ready to break open
and receive yourself
to yourself.

A poem is the whisper
that tells everything,
the secret that cannot be denied:

You are exactly as
you've always been—
Beloved Word,
Spoken Self,
Relieved Ache,
Tender Child.

The poem is you.
It always was.

1

WHAT IS RESISTANCE?

Resistance always begins with curiosity, with questions. We often do not ask our questions, not because we are afraid of the answer, but because there might not be a clear answer waiting, or because our communities have taught us that questions are a sign of weakness.

So what is resistance?

The scientific term *resistance* refers to a force, such as friction, that operates opposite the direction of motion of a body and tends to prevent or slow down the body's motion. It is a measure of the degree to which a substance impedes the flow of electric current induced by a voltage.

Resistance is measured in ohms, named after German physicist Georg Ohm, who studied the relationship between voltage, currents, and resistance.

For the purpose of this book, I'd like us to understand resistance as the way we use our everyday lives to exert energy against the dangerous status quo of our time. But resistance cannot only be about what we are against. When we choose to resist something or someone, we are also choosing something else on the other side. Perhaps we are choosing ourselves; perhaps we are choosing an inclusive love or a more just society. We resist ableism or racism because we know there is a better way—this is the way resistance works, and we must both find and create that better way together.

This chapter is about questions as resistance, which leads us to ideas of deconstruction and evolution. We begin to recognize these currents in our lives, not by ohms, but by the change we notice in ourselves as we choose love and solidarity, as we *resist hate*. But it must begin with us, in our Personal Realm of resistance. It must begin with our questions.

The fear is in that in-between space of not knowing, the emptiness where we have to wait for an uncomfortably long time to come to any sort of conclusion about who we are or what sort of world we live in. Often, it's not at all about the answers but about our willingness to step outside of what we know and ask the question in the first place.

This first realm we find ourselves in is an important one—foundational even. That doesn't mean we always live in the Personal Realm, but this time of going inward, of showing love for ourselves, saying as Lizzo sings, "I'm my own soulmate," takes a lot of courage and a lot of time, and our questions are always a part of that resistance work.

Think of five questions you are holding inside yourself right now. They can be about anything. Here are a few of mine: What does true solidarity require of me? How can I make my front porch more welcoming? How should I navigate social media in a healthier way? What plants do I want in my spring garden? How can I tangibly let my kids know I love them?

1. How can I be a good + respectful ally?
2. Who am I truly?
3. Am I going to be able to make it through my classes?

4. How do I love myself first?
5. How do I know if friends will be lifelong?

In the past, I had questions like, Why am I so scared all the time? Is God really this patriarchal guy with a gavel and a list of my sins, waiting in heaven to damn me to hell? What lies have I believed about my body? (I am *still* asking these questions! That is the journey.)

Curiosity takes root in us as children; I truly believe that. But as we get older, we are taught to trade curiosity for security, and often that security is baked into the status quo of society, of capitalism, which in reality is anything but secure for many of us. Instead of engaging with Mother Earth and the creatures around us, we are taught to commodify the land. We are taught to trust our religious leaders, parents, and teachers more than our own sacred instincts. As a result, we stop listening to our gut, to our hearts, to our own knowing. As Sadhguru writes in his book *Karma*, "We have frittered away our freedom, bartered and sold it to external authorities, whether parental, religious, cultural, or political. Instead of exercising the freedom of consciousness, of choice, we have bought into the voices that have told us that to be human is to be limited, even sinful."[1] I learned in sixth grade how to balance a checkbook, but I was never truly taught how to speak with our nonhuman relatives in a sustainable and relational way.

So as adults, many of us on the path of healing are realizing that we must reclaim our curiosity toward ourselves and the land around us; we must start asking questions we didn't ask before. As we do so, things begin shifting, and, naturally, resistance follows. For many of us, this is also where we begin the journey of deconstruction. This questioning and deconstruction journey can be difficult and messy, but it is a start, and it is holy work, even if in the end we no longer believe what we believed before.

intuition

sometimes can be scary

I have been taught to not question christian works/texts (the Bible)

I have experienced different seasons, different layers of deconstruction throughout my life. In college, I took a world literature class that burst the small evangelical bubble I'd experienced growing up and helped me (painfully) realize that the holy texts I took literally are not holy to everyone but are complex works of literature to read, examine, and critique when possible. My Jewish friends have taught me that their sacred texts also matter to them *because* they can fight with the texts, ask questions, and go on a journey with themselves and the Sacred. But because I did not grow up knowing much about critique or critical thinking, I was scared of opening up my worldview in some ways. But once I did, I found it liberating.

Later, I began a major in social work that forced me into powerful, nuanced conversations about culture, trauma, belief, sexual orientation, poverty, and so much more. The questions that had been buried deep inside me began to rise to the surface and ended up becoming the beautiful beginnings of my deconstruction journey, the chance to ask questions and along the way to critique my childhood faith and my experiences in America, and to ask what my story means to me.

The word *story* is defined as "an account of past events in someone's life or in the evolution of something."[2] I think about this a lot when I travel and speak: How does our story evolve, change, and become? How do we ask questions, and what happens when our questions change over time? If a story is meant to evolve, then so are we. We get to examine our own stories and ask those questions; we get to acknowledge the ways we've changed over the years.

But often, this can be painful. The pain is why many of us choose not to go deeply into the work. If we understand how we got here, then we understand all that went wrong. We understand how people who should have loved us well didn't. And we understand how institutions that should have protected us chose not to. It's why so many of us go to therapy or find chosen family in order to love and be loved out in the world. I think of my queer kin, who fight again and again to exist in spaces where they are loved just as they are.

Julie Rodgers writes about this so viscerally in her book *Outlove*. She asks, "What's a queer person to do in that situation, when the only people we've ever known and loved believe our love is disordered and our bodies are broken?"[3]

What do we do when we realize that the status quo of our religion, our country, our families, or our institutions is to shame those who are queer, trans, Indigenous, Asian, Black, Latinx, poor, Jewish, Sikh, or anything else considered "other" to them? Either we disappear into the toxicity of assimilation completely (or as much as is allowed by society), or we begin to untangle the horrible webs of hate that have for years made us hate our own beloved bodies and experiences.

So we take a step back and ask what our stories mean. We ask how we must now evolve to get to the heart of who we are. We ask what resistance feels like for us. Often, it is through deconstruction. For some, it is through decolonizing. It means taking a look at the systems, and sometimes the people, that would not acknowledge us as fully human and saying that there is a better way to be in this world. It means saying that we are willing to dream and fight for that better way. It means that white folks step back and learn how to listen to those who have been marginalized by our society at every level.

For author and activist Austen Hartke, deconstruction and decolonization involve helping the church understand how it can value and love transgender people. Austen writes, "When a church is trans-affirming, transgender Christians can show up as themselves, unapologetically. By doing that, they show everyone else in the congregation that it's all right to bring their whole selves into the community, that nobody has to 'fake it 'till you make it' as a perfect Christian."[4]

Deconstruction, through honest questions and critiques, is resistance because it not only involves our stories but actually involves *us* and the ways we hold space for our own sacredness. For many queer, nonbinary, two-spirit, and transgender individuals, American and Christian institutions are not safe places, so they know they cannot show up fully as they are. A 2021 report by the Human Rights Campaign found that "fatal violence disproportionately affects transgender women of color—particularly Black transgender women—and that the intersections of racism, sexism, homophobia, biphobia, transphobia and unchecked access to guns conspire to deprive them of employment, housing, healthcare and other necessities."[5]

These acts of violence toward transgender and gender-nonconforming people are to the detriment of us all—when our spaces limit us, we cannot practice our humanity fully. We are colonized and trapped in cycles of oppression, and the way out is through storytelling and love, through those who, as Austen reminds us, show up fully as themselves until we all learn to do so. People who have been forced to the margins of our society are so often our prophets and theologians, the ones who point us toward God—the Sacred—and toward a better way of being human. In the Personal Realm, let's remember those who have helped us ask difficult questions, who have helped us love ourselves well.

What I have come to realize is that theologians—people who are looking to understand God or the Divine—are people who have been asking difficult questions for years and grounding themselves in the reality that it is both lifelong work and fully sacred. They also happen to be great storytellers. So when I am confused about what part of the journey I am on (Am I deconstructing or decolonizing? Am I reconstructing or floating about in space?), I look to the storytellers to remind me that it's okay to be wherever I am. I write this book to remind you that it's okay to be wherever you are. As Mia Birdsong writes, "All of us have something to shed, something to purge, so we can make room for the reclamation and reinvention of community and family."[6]

Every few years, it seems there are folks within Christianity who rise up and declare that deconstruction is harmful and only leads people away from their churches into an unsafe world. First, this puts a substantial emphasis on the church's success at helping people navigate the world in a loving, kind way, <u>which is not often the case</u>. Second, folks who say this have little faith in those of us who have left the institutional church to find Creator where Creator has always been—*everywhere, especially in the places the church told us God was not.*

yes ↖

← *have been feeling this a lot lately*

My experience with deconstructing the faith I grew up with and examining my own story and evolution has led me to more questions, to more love, and to a fuller experience of the Divine. Has it caused me to question and distrust powerful people and institutions? Yes. That's why it's so scary for those institutions. And yet so many of us who are asking deep, difficult questions about the ways in which we grew up find that, yes, the world can be scary, but it can also be beautiful. And journeying out to find it all, to break free of the barriers set on us by institutions, governments, and religious leaders, *is* resistance.

RESISTANCE COMMITMENT: Examine your own story. Where, when, and how have you deconstructed? Name some ways that you're still questioning something today, and give yourself permission to ask those questions for however long you need to ask them. This is your life you're dealing with. Deal gently.

2

ART AS RESISTANCE

I know the irony of bringing this book into the world during the time we are living in. As I write, COVID-19 is still ravaging much of the world, and in America people are dying, many unvaccinated, from a horrific virus that we still don't fully understand, and many Americans are fighting over mask mandates and vaccines. Afghan people are trying to flee their country and continue to encounter a world that doesn't want to shelter them. Haiti is reeling from an earthquake that has killed thousands, and racism and discrimination rise to the surface around us. Voting rights and the rights to body autonomy are suppressed in the United States. Russia is invading Ukraine. Roe v. Wade has been overturned by the Supreme Court and the right to guns is valued over the right to care for our own bodies. The world feels like a terrifying place. It is difficult to write about *resistance* when we are all so weary in every way imaginable, and yet that's exactly where resistance matters.

Let's take a breath here and remember our medicine, these words that guide us: **I am a human being. I am always arriving.**

When COVID-19 was just hitting us in 2020, I was on Instagram a lot, because that seemed to be where the artists were. One afternoon, I sat on my living room couch watching a live performance of Irish singer-songwriter Glen Hansard from his kitchen as he sipped red wine and chatted with his neighbor. Artist and author Morgan Harper Nichols shared her art with us, words and images that brought us home to ourselves. Somehow, I felt the utter heaviness of the time we'd found ourselves in and a deep gratitude that we were opening up our most creative parts to one another, those parts that said, "Even though the world is heavy and we are in so much pain, we still create *with and for each other*, because we belong to one another." Dave Matthews put on a live Twitter concert, mentioning how much he's learned from the Indigenous people in his life. Poets read poetry, authors read children's books to the kids stuck at home, others shared their art in live demonstrations, and musicians produced new content for their online spaces. Some of us didn't create a single thing, so we drew from the well of others who could. *Art is living resistance.*

When the world is heavy with grief and unanswered questions, art is undoubtedly important. It points us toward resistance. In the spring of 2021, a show that greatly impacted my life and my ideas of resistance debuted on television: *Rutherford Falls*. It tells the story of Nathan Rutherford, a white man descended from the settlers of the small town of Rutherford Falls, and Reagan Wells, an Indigenous woman descended from the tribal nation that lived on the land for centuries and continues to live there. It is a complex, nuanced show about the stories we tell, including the lies and the truths, and how they get mingled into our everyday experiences.

What makes *Rutherford Falls* so powerful is that it tells an Indigenous story, and it is Indigenous folks, from the production room to the writing team, who are giving content and perspective throughout. It is the first show I have ever seen with an Indigenous woman as the star. Sierra Teller Ornelas, Ed Helms, and

31

at the end of the day we are all human beings

Michael Schur are the creators, and you can feel the presence of the Indigenous scriptwriters as the show unfolds. I took to Twitter and interviewed a few of them—Jana Schmieding, who plays Reagan; Michael Greyeyes, who plays Terry; and of course Sierra, the series showrunner. We chatted about the power of this moment and the excitement that lies ahead as other shows, like *Reservation Dogs*, continue to bring Indigenous realities, drama, and laughter to the screen. *Rutherford Falls* and the continued representation of Indigenous people on screen reminds me that I can exist fully as I am today without apology.

Perhaps, at the end of the day, that is what art does for us: it puts our complexities and nuances on display, and reveals parts of our human nature, our sacredness, that we didn't know were there before. Art as resistance reminds all of us that the boxes we are so often put into don't always define us, even if they are helpful tools to align ourselves. Refusing to be placed in a box someone else creates for us is not to remain elusive but to simply acknowledge that who we are is not simple—it is an act of decolonization. Maybe that's the gift we give one another: to remember our complexities through the art we create and the spaces we inhabit.

It may seem silly, but the old Disney musical *The Newsies* makes me cry every single time I watch it. I grew up with a *Newsies* cassette tape and have had the songs memorized for years. In high school, I performed a debate about the Newsboys' fight against corporate publisher Pulitzer and Hearst. But when I watched it with my six-year-old for the first time a few years ago, it brought the story to life for me as I saw my own kid witnessing these other children from New York fighting for their rights.

Our family has had conversations about labor unions and why resistance matters, and in that moment at the end of the movie when the newsies are unsure if any other kids are going to show up, suddenly the floodgates open—*I remember why it all matters.*

representation is SO important

It matters that workers at Starbucks, Apple, and Amazon are rallying together to demand better work environments, fighting corporations that threaten their livelihood when they should be the ones providing it. I remember why resistance is as much about the fight as it is about the art. Of course, not all resistance movements come with song and dance, but I have witnessed resistance in the form of art so many times and continue to live inspired by the artists who create for the sake of a better future.

At the beginning of this book, I quote the Foo Fighters' song "The Best of You," in which they ask, "Were you born to resist / Or be abused?" Art is about voice, and as much as it can be about violence or hate, it can be about the personal and communal ways we fight or rage against the status quo of hate, as we've witnessed throughout the centuries. Art changes us.

In an article in *Grassroots Journal*, Sydney Stevenson writes, "Using art as a nonviolent form of protest can carry immense meaning and strength, connecting people through their resistance."[1] Art brings us alive to issues we may have overlooked before. In the disabilities community, DisArt was born out of helping communities understand that "expressions of a disability culture can transform communities from awareness, to understanding, to belonging, ensuring the full and equitable participation of all disabled people."[2] Through journals, podcast episodes, current news, and more, they are using art to bring able-bodied people to an awareness of the experiences, cultures, and passions of the disabled community. Art connects us, teaches us, and yes, shows us how to resist. In the coming years, as organizations and groups want to be back in person together, our job is to ask how art and the events centered on that art can continue to be accessible to everyone who needs it.

Another example of art as resistance is the raised fist, a symbol and action that has been around for centuries both in artwork and in protests all over the world. When I titled this book, I knew that any ideas of resistance or activism would likely bring to mind

i never realized how important art is, but it makes a ton of sense

in this world everything becomes a trend

this symbol, because of its power. Today you can find some form of the raised fist on numerous book covers and in other forms of artwork, such as bumper stickers and memes. Like so much art, our job is to examine how art transforms over time, to look at where such symbols were born and what they have become today. Niela Orr wrote about the raised fist in 2017 when Donald Trump was president: "In a world that appropriates and mutates every symbol until it's reduced to a sad, emojified shadow of its former self, how will this vital symbol of strength in the face of oppression (or even total annihilation) retain its intensity? The hope is that it does not become just another peace sign or smiley face, the kind of symbol that adorns Mini Cooper bumpers and preteen earrings."[3]

The raised fist has taken quite a journey: from the art of the Taller de Gráfica Popular (People's Graphic Workshop) in 1937 Mexico to Tommie Smith and John Carlos raising their fists during the 1968 Olympic National Anthem ceremony to Trump raising his fist in his many white supremacist, racist, xenophobic speeches. Knowing the symbol's history forces us to ask the questions that Orr asks: What does sending a raised fist emoji to a friend in a text mean today, and how can we embody solidarity in more realistic ways? What will it mean to future generations?

To be artists in the world means asking how our craft shapes and shifts over time. If my writing is truly based in resistance, then I must pay attention to how words are used both to harm and to hold up in solidarity. Even a short tweet holds great power, and over the years, I've recognized that. Creating online spaces that hold the reality of both fierce truth-telling and gentleness is difficult to accomplish, but nuance allows us to live our fully human experience and resist in ways that will last. Our art is our resistance in every way possible, and it brings us home to ourselves when we feel lost.

My father was in a rock band in high school. Growing up, I always cherished hearing him play guitar, his tenor voice bringing '80s rock and love songs into the air around us. He made a cassette tape of some of his music that I listened to for years. After my parents divorced when I was nine, the music left our house. It even left the house where my dad began living in Oklahoma as he lost his own art and music to pain and trauma. The air had suddenly changed. It took me a few years to pick up a guitar again myself, to lean into the art of music and words that existed within the void my dad had left.

I carried so much pain and hurt from my father leaving, and yet the music connected me to him, healed me from the brokenness, and held me when things were too hard to put into spoken words. Singing and poetry were my medicine, and they have continued to be my medicine of resistance ever since. Music helps me slow down, pause, and pay attention to my own soul and the world around me, and words are a consistent balm.

In my early thirties, I learned that I function best in my work and life when I have slow mornings that include words and music guiding me into the day. So after we wake up and get the kids off to school, my partner Travis and I have our morning coffee together. We talk for a while, and he sets off to work, and then I sink into a good book for a bit. When that time is up, I transition to writing, or maybe studying the Potawatomi language through an online course I have used for a few years. Often I play the piano, even though piano was never really *my* instrument.

But that changed when we moved to New England in 2020. The house we were renting in a rural Vermont town had a piano in the living room, an old one that was slightly out of tune, and absolutely beautiful. One afternoon I decided to teach myself some basic chords so I could play music that I love—holiday songs in the winter, Coldplay for my kids, jazz for myself. I caught on quicker than I expected, and I fell in love immediately with the way my soul felt when I played, a release of stressful energy, an easing of my anxiety, leaning into the beauty of song. I played nearly every day that we lived in Vermont for those eleven months, and then we moved to a new city and I left that piano behind.

A few months into living in Philadelphia, my partner took me to a store that sells refurbished pianos, and I found the one for me right away. It was delivered a few weeks later, and those teary-eyed moments of longing for a chance to play dissipated as I sat down to sing.

Having that time to play in the morning, if only for fifteen to thirty minutes, grounds me for the work ahead, reminding me why art matters for embodying the work of resistance. When we lived in Vermont, my children found music to be a lifeline. On the drives to and from school, we'd listen to our "Native playlist"—a string of songs on my YouTube account, from Frank Waln to Taboo to Buffy Sainte-Marie and everything in between. A favorite song was Taboo's collaboration with IllumiNative and Mag7, "One World," which celebrates the power of coming together, no matter who we are or what we embody. For my kids, that season of living in rural Vermont reminded them of who they are and what kind of world they want to be a part of creating as they grow up.

Art isn't just for entertainment; it's also a way of being in the world. As we engage within the Personal Realm, our focus is on how resistance works in our personal lives. This happens on the macro and the micro level, inviting creativity on every spectrum. So however you are an artist (and yes, you are, whether you realize it or not), your art can help you process the world. Asha Frost, an Indigenous author and medicine woman, writes in her book *You Are the Medicine*, "The Fire is lit. The Ancestors are here. Your Medicine is calling. Let us open our space."[4] Asha holds space for others to curiously engage their own healing medicine. Her words and spirit are resistance, reminding us that our best art, our best creations, start when we light our own fires, when we let our ancestors speak to us, when we show up with our own medicine.

Living resistance is also being critical about the art that we consume. For instance, we can ask questions about the arts and crafts our children make in their classrooms around Thanksgiving, or we can pay attention to the racist origins of the song "Jingle Bells."[5] Since it is our work to deconstruct, to ask questions of what we have been given or of the art we consume, we must pay attention to what our art invokes in the world. Even as I write this book, I am heavy with concern for the way my words land out there with all of you. Does my art reflect the spirit of resistance and solidarity that I hope for? Where am I missing it? Where does my own art fall short, and where does it spark beautiful, needed change in others and in myself?

Art heals us, both individually and communally. But for our own sake, art is a tether, a reminder of what resistance means for our personal lives. Throughout history, peoples have expressed who they are through art—stories, paintings, carvings, statues and sculptures, music. Art is literally everything that we are, and when things are hard, art holds us together.

RESISTANCE COMMITMENT: Explore art in a new way. Find or create a piece of artwork that expresses resistance in some way, and put it where it can speak to you often. Watch a new series, documentary, or movie that challenges your assumptions and helps you ask better questions.

3

PRESENCE
AS RESISTANCE

The next three chapters of the Personal Realm focus on presence, embodiment, and radical self-love. Each plays a role in our everyday lives and therefore in our resistance. They are connected, yet they are also separate; they build on one another. As an Indigenous woman—as a Potawatomi *kwe*—I have found that practicing presence with myself and Earth has led me to embodiment and the radical act of self-love. I live in the spirit of Anishinaabe author Leanne Betasamosake Simpson's words: "I need to place my emotional experience, my life, in a position of honor. I need to respect and listen to my intelligence as a cisgender Indigenous woman and as an Indigenous person. As *kwe*."[1]

Our practices of presence, embodiment, and radical self-love as resistance will take shape depending on where we are in time and space. If we come from oppressed or marginalized peoples and histories, if we carry intergenerational trauma, then we, and perhaps even our families, will need to pursue healing as part of our work. When we lean into what presence, embodiment, and radical self-love ask of us, we understand on a new level their importance for us and for those who come after us.

As we lean into these next chapters in the Personal Realm, consider what the practices of presence, embodiment, and radical self-love mean in your own life. Go gentle. Take deep breaths. Visit with your child self often. Let's start by leaning into *presence*.

When I was in high school, two classes deeply impacted me: Intro to Psychology and Creative Writing: Poetry. Together, these classes brought me to the realization that I love people and words and that I wanted my life to be about both.

The struggle with this reality came during college, when I began to understand that I couldn't separate the two. As I took psychology courses, I was also taking a class on Russian author Dostoevsky; while I studied social work, I kept studying world literature and taking creative writing courses.

As I studied people and their ways of living and healing in my social work classes, I couldn't decide which was more important to me: the macro, large-scale way of experiencing things or the micro, individual understanding of humanity. I was constantly caught in a cycle of in-between, of moving back and forth between these different and seemingly opposite spaces.

I didn't understand how a love for all this could possibly work in my life. But I also kept being drawn toward people and words, seeing the whole and seeing each person beneath each decision made. The macro *and* the micro were important to me. I couldn't choose one or the other.

Fast forward to this moment in my life: I am an award-winning author, poet, and public speaker. I write on identity, spirituality, self-love, self-care, and what it means to be human. I am still, constantly, falling more in love with people and with words.

I now understand why I couldn't separate the things I loved or the different ways of understanding the world. Now I know that to love other humans, their liminal spaces and stories, their cultures, their identities and religions, is to love myself too. And the best way for me to express that interconnectedness is through words, images, poetry, and story. I now understand that to get to the macro, we have to spend time in the micro; to understand how we got here as a whole, we have to understand who we are, each one of us, and the stories we tell. The liminal space is where we live.

I may not fully understand the human mind, but I understand grief and joy, the ebb and flow of both throughout the seasons of our lives, and I cannot escape the various ways liminal space is a constant part of us. So I write. And as I write, I believe in Us—the whole, connected Us—because we are here on Earth to be connected to ourselves, one another, and all the creatures we encounter along the path of our lives.

Presence is about recognizing our relationship to ourselves and one another. Potawatomi author and scientist Robin Wall Kimmerer puts it like this: "The land is the real teacher. All we need as students is mindfulness. Paying attention is a form of reciprocity with the living world, receiving the gifts with open eyes and open heart."[2]

What do we learn from this wisdom? We learn that reciprocity is resistance. That mindfulness is resistance. That paying attention to the land is resistance, and it leads us deeper into relationship with all things and all beings.

I keep a begonia plant in my office, on my desk by the window. It's thriving in that spot, right beside the bright light that filters in through the blue curtain in the afternoon. I have learned to care for begonias because I have killed a few in my time, and every time it is painful to admit that I could not keep them alive and well.

When this begonia plant flourishes, I am full of hope. But still, sometimes I notice that they are thirsty. I pour water from my own drinking glass into the plastic container beneath the pot, so their roots can drink first. Within seconds, the water disappears, and I say to myself, "Oh, you were so thirsty."

They keep drinking and blooming and asking for more care in that most gentle way plants do, and I say that I am sorry when they are too thirsty or too drenched in sunlight.

And I wonder how thirsty we are, or if we notice, if that mindfulness and way of keeping watch happens in our own souls. I wonder if we let others know when we need a drink or a break from the heat, or that we might need a little deadheading here or there. And when we get closer to the water, we drink it up within seconds, begging for more, while nearby someone says, "Oh, Love, you were so thirsty."

I wonder if we even notice that we're thirsty.

One morning on the drive to school, my oldest son got frustrated because he wanted to read a comic book and at the same time sing along to "Seagulls! (Stop It Now)" by Bad Lip Reading. "I want to learn how to multitask!" he proclaimed from the back seat. I laughed, thinking about moments when I was younger and wanted to challenge my brain to do a few things at once. But as an adult, I have more moments when, instead, I long to be able to focus singularly on one thing and focus on it well, though this often doesn't happen. Most of the time, I'm trying to manage multiple tasks or ideas at once, never fully focused on any one of them. It leaves me feeling overwhelmed.

I fold the laundry, but I watch something on Netflix while I do it. I work, but I listen to music too. I often think about mindfulness and how it shows up in my everyday life, and I've realized it's often about the possibility of stopping to notice the bite of food we just ate and the plant we are tending to, a spiritual consciousness that keeps us tethered to the world around us. This is a difficult thing to practice.

When I was young, I'd come home from school, get a snack, and do my homework in front of the television while I watched a favorite show or movie. I got my work done, and I was a good

i struggle w/ this a lot

student, but I wasn't living fully present to anything—to the sounds or sights around me, to my own mind's ability to create, to the afternoon light streaming through the bedroom window.

Learning to step back from multitasking teaches me better what kinship is—to be aware and connected to that chickadee on my back deck, those begonias on the windowsill, the vegetables in my meal. Everything is relationship; everything is connected. I want my children to learn *that* instead.

There's plenty of research on the harms of multitasking, especially in the technology-addicted reality we are living in. A *Psychology Today* article mentions ten real risks of multitasking, including harm to our brains, increase in chronic stress, and becoming less efficient.[3] When I sit down to write, I often set a timer for myself—twenty minutes of writing with no social media. (And no, I *never* break my own rule [insert side-eye emoji here].)

Presence is resistance, in almost every way we can imagine—presence to ourselves, presence to each other, presence to whatever we should be paying attention to in that moment. Mystics of every religion have written on this because they knew why it mattered then and why it matters now. For us to be fully alive, we must be present, and when we are, we resist hate in ourselves and in the world around us. I practice presence with my children because I know I wasn't always given presence. I hope to heal something in the work of presence, and to watch as that healing ripples out into the lives of others around me.

One day after reading about presence and mindfulness, I sat down to eat my lunch of water and frozen organic burritos, and instead of eating while scrolling social media posts, I sat still for a minute and paid attention to my food. I noticed the beans, the rice, the processed cheese I'd dumped on top of those burritos. I could hear my Weimaraner, Jupiter, struggling to get comfortable at my feet. I saw sunlight shining through the window. I took a sip of water and thought, "Water is life. Really. It is."

What overwhelmed me in that moment was this deep sense of gratitude for the sunlight, my dog, that burrito, the lack of Twitter. It wasn't just a mental "let's practice gratitude" but a spiritual reorientation to a living connectedness, a chance to remember how and why I am in relation to the food I eat, the animals I care for, the water I drink, the sunlight that never ceases to shine on me. *This is resistance*, I decided, a singular focus of mind and spirit in this moment that deflects the status quo of violence as connection and instead begs for another way. Gardening teaches me the same kind of presence and connectedness—noticing and tending to these beings who are my friends and kin, who provide for me and allow me to see their flourishing. Presence means living into resistance in the most organic and connected way, the way of being alive, being human, even if your presence is practiced toward a frozen burrito and a snoring dog.

i love this mindset

Since my earliest years, I have been a very ritualistic person. Whether I understood it as ritual or not, I enjoyed having space to honor things in myself and around me. The more I became embedded in the Southern Baptist tradition of the faith I was raised in, the more I wandered from that ritualistic way of being. Ritual is allowed in the church but only in ways that fit, that are part of the atonement process to cleanse our souls from sin and embrace a certain kind of community. As much as I wanted to be close to God, I also lacked that closeness because I knew only a colonized version of God that did not value all of my questions or the nonlinear way I wanted to understand the world around me.

In the last few years I have come back to ritual again but in my own way this time. I honor the seasons and cycles the way my Potawatomi ancestors did. I allow myself to process on a cyclical timeline instead of a linear one. I take breaks to honor rest, and work to decolonize the aspects of my spirituality that clamp down on my questions. Nap Ministry founder Tricia Hersey writes about the importance of rest: "My rest as a Black woman in America suffering from generational exhaustion and racial trauma always was a political refusal and social justice uprising within my body. I took to rest and naps and slowing down as a way to save my life, resist the systems telling me to do more and most importantly as a remembrance to my Ancestors who had their DreamSpace stolen from them. This is about more than naps."[4]

Tricia knows that naps (and cycles of rest that buck the status quo of white supremacy) are resistance and ritual, that they save us, hold us, and give something back to us when we are weary from colonization, racism, white supremacy, and hate.

One afternoon in early winter, I felt this ache that I couldn't put words to. I knew I was grieving—specifically, grieving things I'd lost in the last year or two. I was grieving all that the pandemic took from us; I was grieving the loss of our dog, Sam, who we had since before Travis and I got married and who died while we were living in Vermont; I was grieving the change of other relationships. I needed space to honor the changes.

So I went into my office, closed the door, and lit a few candles. I placed them on the floor and sat down, bringing strips of paper and a pen along with me. I took my time, letting the tears come, letting myself feel whatever I needed to feel. I was angry. I was so sad that it felt like I couldn't breathe. I was also somehow grateful. I wrote down the things I'd lost on the first strips of paper, honoring each one slowly, naming them to myself.

Then I moved to the next pile of papers, where I wrote something I'd gained. We'd lost our dog, Sam, but gained a new puppy named Blaze. I'd lost relationships, but I'd gained other ones, as well as a better sense of myself. I said goodbye to the season before and welcomed in the season here and the season to come. I cried more. I took deep breaths until my body's systems found their grounding. I honored everything that is sacred about hurting and healing and not knowing what comes next.

> Living resistance is about letting ourselves hurt and heal, without knowing what comes next in a society that tells us we should shut off our emotions and always have a plan.

That day, it was necessary that I stop and engage with where I was. If I hadn't, I would have kept it balled up inside until it inevitably worked its way out, eventually, in ways that might have ended up harming me and the people I love. Ritual helps us practice recovery and pay attention to the space our soul is inhabiting. Suleika Jaouad writes about her recovery from a horrific diagnosis of cancer in her breathtaking book *Between Two Kingdoms*. When processing the aftermath of the cancer, the part where she must enter the world of healing again, she writes, "Recovery is not about salvaging the old at all. It's about accepting that you must forsake a familiar self forever, in favor of the one that is being newly born. It is an act of brute, terrifying discovery."[5]

Recovery and discovery both require presence, and more often than not, those spaces require some sort of ritual. Suleika's ritual (and her understanding of moving between realms) was a road trip across the country to visit a number of people she respected and loved—it was a giant ritual of gratitude, requiring presence and, yes, resistance to the status quo that would have her believe that pushing away the fear of the unknown is what is best.

When I enter into ritual or ceremony, I am reminding myself that it matters to be present to the human experience. It matters to let the mystical and sacred pull us out of ourselves in ways we don't understand, through a lit candle and a piece of scrap paper, through a song and a howling cry, through a dance or the echoing silence of being alone and letting the soul speak.

Ritual, paying attention, and being present, it's all resistance, and it all teaches me that the human journey matters.

RESISTANCE COMMITMENT: Create a new ritual for yourself. Maybe it involves candles or drinking a glass of cool water or a cup of hot tea. Maybe it's based on a breathing exercise or speaking kindness over yourself. Whatever it is, commit to practicing this ritual a few times each week, and see what you learn about being present to yourself.

4

EMBODIMENT
AS RESISTANCE

As we shift our discussion from presence to embodiment, it's helpful to ask, What is the difference between presence and embodiment in the Personal Realm of resistance?

Hillary McBride writes in her book *The Wisdom of Your Body*, "The body is central to our experiences, to our sense of ourselves, to our autobiographical narratives. The body is the only way we have to move through life."[1] I consider presence to be the noticing and the paying attention, and I believe it is an essential step *toward embodiment*. Embodiment is what comes with presence, with acknowledgment perhaps of grief or trauma, or an understanding of who we are in the world.

About two years into therapy, I realized that I love reading and thinking about how to manage my anxiety or my journey with grief. But I also realized that I tend to take in the information only as far as it seeps into my brain. I often do not, in any real way, *embody* the grief or the practices that I need to experience real change. Embodiment is difficult for those of us who grew up in spiritual traditions that made us deeply aware of our bodies and at the same time ashamed of them. The evangelical purity movement that I lived through in my teenage years profoundly shaped the way I understood my body and, coupled with other layers of trauma that I carried, led to what I can only describe as a lingering and growing distance from myself, near total disembodiment.

In my late twenties I began to notice pain in my body, and I soon realized that it was associated with trauma responses from when I was young. *Why does my stomach or lower back hurt in a certain way when I'm thinking about this experience? Why do I get headaches or mentally freeze up in certain situations?* I was beginning to understand that my body is a beautiful, vast system of communication that I need to pay attention to.

I am still on a journey of embodiment. As an Indigenous woman, overcoming the misogyny and colonization of the purity movement *is resistance in every way.* The embodiment journey is lifelong, as Dr. McBride will tell you. Many of us will be forever learning to ask our bodies questions in order to listen better. Sometimes it begins with deep breaths, exercise, or screaming when we need to scream. Sometimes it happens through dance or poetry or other forms of art. Embodiment is taking what we didn't understand or regaining what was lost so that we can learn to be present to our own stories again. And that is exactly what the world needs—more embodied people helping one another practice embodiment.

I recently attended a series of strength training classes, and while I was enjoying using weights for the strength training, I suddenly stumbled into a class that did not involve weights; it was a class involving only our *bodies.* The instructor, more than once, pointed out that our bodies are made for resistance, and that really challenged me. Before we pick up the weights or add to the workout routines, do we trust that the very bodies we are given to live in every single day are *made for living resistance?* Do

Embodiment is about naming and paying attention. As I've shared in the last few chapters, it has taken me years to understand my own body (and I'm still learning), to let it speak to me and to be present to its rhythms and voice. Part of this journey has been about recognizing and naming my own daily journey with anxiety. In 2021, I wrote an essay about what anxiety *feels like* in my body through an experience at a river with my family, and I want to share it with you as we ask what resistance looks like in our bodies today. Here's the essay:

We have a river running through our backyard.

For the average kayaker or summer swimmer, this isn't remarkable, but it is for me. It's remarkable for me to live by water because water is sacred and because I have an immense fear of it.

I write in my book *Native: Identity, Belonging, and Rediscovering God* that when I was a child, I fell under water at a hotel pool and was rescued by my older sister. I'm not sure if that one moment could have shaped an entire life of fear, or if it was just a general anxious fear of everything unknown around me, but my entire life I've been scared of water—scared of drowning, scared of my kids drowning, scared of my partner drowning.

A month or so before we moved away from Atlanta, we visited a spot on the Chattahoochee River where people bring their dogs to run free and play in the water. They fetch sticks and pee by people's bags of food; they run up to strangers and look panicky when they think they've lost their family members. For the dogs, this area is a giant water-playground, and we are the bystanders who see them come alive.

One day we took our kayak out to the river, just to test it on the current. Travis took it out right away, all around this small island and back again to us. I wondered how enjoyable it was, or if I could ever be brave enough to try. We decided to trek across the water with our kids so they could play on some large rocks, but I could feel my anxiety rising with every step as the water got deeper.

I stayed back on a large rock while they went ahead to play. I watched them, their joy, their wonderment, and I sat quietly with my own stress and my own *want* to feel joy. *How did this become my reality?* I wondered. But I watched them. I watched Travis teach them to trust and stay safe on the current, to move from rock to rock with confidence.

I watched and asked myself more questions. I couldn't trust my body or mind to get me there, so I felt stuck and uneasy. I was missing a moment, and I'd never get it back.

I'm learning how anxiety works. Sometimes it feels like a pulsing sensation; it moves from being faint to being so loud that I cannot ignore it, and it causes me to lose sleep and breathe so shallow I can't get through to myself or anyone else. Other times it's like a glass box that I am stuck inside of, and the only way out is to climb through the top. But there are magic things to do to escape, magic things that reveal a hidden ladder I can use to climb up and out and to the ones I love.

That day on the river, I stayed inside the glass box for a while. I watched our kids, grateful that they were learning outside the realm of fear, and I sat still, asking my questions, talking to my own unsureness. Then Travis told me I should take the kayak out on the water. He told me that *I* should go around that little island, guiding myself through the Chattahoochee's current, making my way around the people and tree branches and rocks along the river's path.

When I'm scared of water, I think back to a summer when I was about thirteen years old at an outdoor church camp. We were in pairs or groups of three and thrust onto a river with a canoe, assured that the short lesson we'd received on the bus ride to the river would be enough to give us a fun and safe adventure.

They were wrong.

We tipped the canoe multiple times because we couldn't communicate with one another and had no idea what we were doing—three teenage girls who were on an outdoor trip, trying to manage their periods, and trying to navigate a river and a river instrument they'd never used before.

I remembered.

I remembered that the way I learned to swim was from my best friend Colleen when I was a teenager in our neighborhood pool. A teenager and I could barely swim, like I can barely swim now.

Maybe fear and anxiety are born in us at some point and then just grow and grow, and along with them, that glass box grows and grows, taller and taller, until the top that we can climb out of becomes so far away we barely know how to even begin the climb, let alone imagine what it feels like on the outside. We see the world go on, and we stay there, alone.

But in that moment, I imagined.

Travis helped me get into the kayak and instructed me on exactly where to go to get around the island.

"Are you sure that's where I go? Do I go around those people this way or the other way? Are there big branches there?" Thirteen-year-old me was asking the questions. Little me was coming out of the hotel pool, asking the questions.

"Trust the water," he said.

"Trust the current, follow it, and it will lead you," he said.

Trust the water.

Trust the water.

Trust the water.

I said it over and over, as I almost ran into a large tree branch, as I maneuvered the kayak to stay with the current's course, as I came around the island and saw my eight-year-old guiding me back.

"You did it, Mom! You did it!"

I was so fully aware of their love and my own box, and that day I nearly climbed out. I was so close to the top, to the outside. For a few minutes, the box didn't seem to exist. I felt happy and strong, like I did a thing that couldn't be done, like I climbed my own small mountain, like I found the magic that unlocks the ladder I use to climb up and up and up.

Trusting the journey of our embodiment is seeking and living resistance.

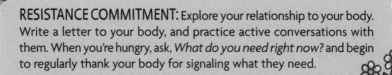

RESISTANCE COMMITMENT: Explore your relationship to your body. Write a letter to your body, and practice active conversations with them. When you're hungry, ask, *What do you need right now?* and begin to regularly thank your body for signaling what they need.

5

RADICAL SELF-LOVE
AS RESISTANCE

I remember the first time I thought about it, this thought that perhaps some of us have considered but not many of us talk about.

What if, when everything is stripped away, I don't actually like myself?

I whispered it inside my head, afraid that someone might hear it if I screamed it. Or maybe God would hear me and confirm that I was either a liar or a silly child, or worse: both.

My most raw thoughts have always come while doing the dishes. When I was a young, acceptable Southern Baptist girl, I'd listen to Sara Groves or Switchfoot CDs from the boom box in the kitchen while washing dishes at my sister Tiffany's house. I'd pray there. I'd dream and imagine. I'd cry. I'd process, all the questions, doubts, and other thoughts shifting around inside my head, all while letting soapy water make the grime disappear before my very eyes.

The scary thought didn't come to me as a kid, though. It happened while I was doing the dishes in our farmhouse in Vermont. We'd just moved a few months earlier. After releasing my second, most vulnerable book during the first few months of COVID-19, I was exhausted. I was determined to say no to things that couldn't help me do my work in a healthy way.

Vermont was a reset button.

I moved to Vermont with this motto: <u>I want to experience my authentic self in the absence of external expectations.</u>

Maybe you need this motto too. Maybe I'm not alone in it.

Except, what happens when external expectations are the way you breathe and live and have your being? What if you've shaped your entire life, and even your idea of God, around an external expectation that you can never outlive? What if God doesn't want our authentic selves and we are stuck washing dishes that never seem to get clean?

What if?

Some of us are never allowed to hit rock bottom. We are the ones who have to keep the family together, keep the parents and teachers happy, keep the pastor nodding in approval. We are not allowed to say, "I've become someone I don't know, and the hole is deep." There are no deep holes in the Christian evangelical faith. There is only heaven or hell and a choice.

Here, though, we are free to explore radical self-love. Radical self-love is not the same as self-care. We talk about self-care a lot. But self-care gets swallowed up by spa days and shopping sprees, and before we know it, it's a buzzword for anything that can be made into a product to be sold—we must *buy* our self-care. That is not what self-care actually is, but that's a conversation for another day. For the sake of this chapter, we are focusing on something else: resistance as radical *self-love*.

I adore the way author Najwa Zebian writes about this in her book *Welcome Home: A Guide to Building a Home for Your Soul*. For her, self-love is a room we must enter within ourselves daily, a place we need to frequent. She writes, "Self-love is an integral part of your everyday life, not a luxury you treat yourself to every once in a while. Put real work into giving yourself what you need."[1]

Entering my early thirties, I'd never examined a great many things—my body's responses to trauma, the ways I was people-pleasing, how I lacked healthy boundaries in my personal and work life, and how I was daily entering a room of self-hate and shame instead of self-love.

But, as she reminds us, whatever room we enter becomes our everyday experience. When I finally got quiet by the sink, doing the dishes, I noticed what was going on inside. I noticed that if all my work and identity markers were stripped away, I was mostly afraid of what I'd find there. I was expecting someone I didn't even like. I was already living in the room of self-hatred, even though that gorgeous room of self-love was right down the hall, full of fresh flowers, welcoming reading chairs, and wide-open windows.

Take a moment to examine this for yourself. Can you begin to pack up and clear out the room of self-hatred and start entering a different room where you are fully your beloved self? It will require time, patience, and grief, but it's worth it to start living a new reality.

Self-love is one of the most important forms of resistance because it is what we begin everything from. If we are doing amazing work in the world yet neglecting ourselves, it's all going to catch up to us sooner or later. This I why I wrote about *presence* and *embodiment* in the previous two chapters—we are building something here, building toward a way of *being* in the world in which we connect and incorporate all parts of who we are into the vision we hold for a better way. *That is, indeed, resistance.*

What happened after I left those dishes in the sink and continued on in the inner world I was unsure of? I ended up finding her—the little girl in me, the woman in me, that authentic self that I wasn't sure was even there. It turns out, I like her—I love

56

her. She's fierce and kind, and when she's paying attention, she creates beautiful things for herself and others.

She grieves for the little girl who got lost all those years ago, and sometimes they hold space for each other:

That girl who had those thoughts buried deep and couldn't even ask them out loud.

That girl who knew God would be angry if the prayer journals weren't full.

That girl who was at home in herself yet far from her self-home, all at the same time.

Today I'm no longer that Southern Baptist evangelical—nor am I even, to many, an "acceptable" Christian. I recognize that I am layered and complex, just as most of us are. Whether I fit the boxes or not, I know that I'm an anomaly to some. So when I do the dishes, I think about that too.

When I do the dishes, I crack open, and whatever spills out is the experience of my authentic self, no matter how painful, with no labels attached. Being able to admit my own fear of not liking myself enough to be alone may be a sign that something is terribly wrong. Or it may be a sign that I've finally given myself permission to hit rock bottom.

Maybe my rock bottom was being surrounded by rivers and mountains, the lands and waters of Vermont that have been tended to by the Abenaki and Wabanaki peoples. Maybe my rock bottom was wiping grime from dishes and taking out the compost. Maybe my rock bottom will always be to finally value myself enough to reconsider what rest might look like and feel like.

This is the journey toward self-love, the journey of living out my resistance.

Decolonization is as much about the micro as it is the macro. We work to change the systems around us by first paying attention to our own surroundings. We meditate, we breathe, we

i need to learn how to set boundaries

contemplate, we find space for self-reflection and communion with Mother Earth because capitalism, patriarchy, and colonialism would have it be otherwise. It is all connected, the micro, the macro, and all the spaces in between.

Having love for ourselves requires boundaries, often in our work, social, and family spheres. In her incredible book *Set Boundaries, Find Peace,* author Nedra Glover Tawwab offers a way forward for those of us who are terrified of standing up for ourselves out in the real world. The subtitle of the book is *A Guide to Reclaiming Yourself,* and that's exactly what boundaries help us do—reclaim ourselves and create better, safer relationships. When we are scared or worried, she suggests reframing how we think about boundaries:

1. Boundaries are a way of advocating for yourself.
2. Boundaries are a way to maintain the health and integrity of a relationship.
3. Boundaries are a way of saying "I love myself."[2]

so big for me

Many of us learned to be afraid of how our relationships will turn out if we enact boundaries, and we learned to give up parts of ourselves in order to maintain "peace" in the process. Radical self-love, this practice of resistance, is *not about being selfish*. It's about honoring our own bodies and spirits, and it's about honoring others by being honest.

Being honest about who we are and what we need is one of the greatest forms of resistance. What would happen if we all lived this way, honest with ourselves, graciously honest with one another? Instead, we are often trapped in patterns of unhealth in various parts of our lives.

As an author and faith leader, I use social media as a necessary tool for my work. But what I've noticed over the years is that social media also adds to my everyday stress in a big way, especially when there is something triggering happening in the news. In 2020, after my book *Native* released, I took a serious look at the way I was using social media.

I deleted Facebook from my phone and began a practice of deleting Twitter from my phone for certain periods of time because the physical act of checking the Twitter app was adding to my stress. It got so bad that some days I would feel jittery from having too much screen time—like my nerve endings were on fire. Indeed, I've had conversations with many friends who are assessing how to use social media in a healthier way, especially when our work is often tied to these toxic spaces. To quote Nedra's book again, "Technology will continue to advance at a rapid rate, so it's necessary to have limits in place to help you protect your happiness and relationships."[3]

Finally, I learned that deleting the apps from my phone for a few days wasn't enough, so now I only use Twitter and Facebook through my computer, and I take regular breaks from Instagram as well. I had to be honest about the effect these spaces have on my body. Setting boundaries has saved my mental and physical health—I can be more present to myself in my everyday life and can inhabit online spaces with more clarity. The changes I've made are connected to both the micro and the macro—how I'm showing up in my own life and in the systems around me in a responsible way.

But it is so difficult to choose rest and self-love, isn't it? I called a friend when I knew that burnout was getting the best of me and I needed a break. I was feeling guilty about stepping back, about going inward for a bit so I could have a wintering season of hibernation and deep soul care. My friend reminded me that rest is not earned but belongs to us, to our bodies, simply because we are human. She encouraged me to hold this space for myself and to not be afraid to share about it, so that others could see what's possible in their own lives and for their own well-being.

Our rest happens in the Personal Realm, but because it is connected to who we are in community, it is also essential within the Communal Realm. We rest as an act of self-love. We rest so that we become more embodied, and in becoming more embodied, we learn to love others better. Rabbi Alan Lew, in his book *This Is Real and You Are Completely Unprepared*, points us toward the idea of rest as an antidote to the hectic busyness that continually threatens to keep us from loving ourselves and one another: "We've become a nation of workaholics, a people who have come to believe that we can conquer death by dint of our own powers, by a ceaseless swirl of activity. To rest is to die, so we never permit ourselves a moment's rest, a moment's *nefresh*, a moment's nothingness."[4]

Nefresh, as Lew shares, can mean nothingness, air, breath, or soul. When we allow ourselves to lean into the nothingness of the inner soul, we are engaging in an act of radical self-love—something our society tends to go against. But people are hungry for rest, for moments of quiet to connect to themselves and to Mother Earth. We must learn what it means to lean into the love that comes from rest and let the effects of that rest ripple beyond ourselves.

As adrienne maree brown writes in *Pleasure Activism*, "We need to learn how to practice love such that care—for ourselves and others—is understood as political resistance and cultivating resilience."[5] I love the connection that brown makes between resistance and resilience. Over the last few years, I have tried not to frame my own life or experiences as resilience, and I think I am starting to realize why: for society (or the oppressor or the colonizer) to tell the oppressed or colonized that we are resilient, even as they continue to knock us down, is entirely a different thing than for the oppressed or colonized to claim our *own resistance on our own terms*.

Does that resonate with anyone?

So how do we reframe our self-love and self-care as both political resistance and cultivated resilience? It becomes this when it belongs *to us*, when we set boundaries around what we need and do not need, when we name what is best for us, and when we reclaim our own sacredness. *That* is the kind of resilience I want to claim and hold on to, the kind my ancestors had, the kind that teaches me embodiment and keeps me dreaming of a better world when things feel so uncertain.

RESISTANCE COMMITMENT: Try taking regular breaks from social media. Every six weeks (or more often if you need to), delete apps from your phone for one full week and see how it feels. The goal isn't to stop using social media when we are overwhelmed but to create regular space to step away so that we gain perspective on the tool and resource it is for us—and learn to use it wisely.

PART 2

THE COMMUNAL REALM

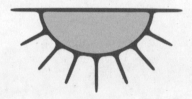

I struggle against colonialism the same way I struggle against depression—by telling myself that I'm not worthless, that I'm not a failure, that things will get better. That every breath I choose to take is a tiny revolution, a rebellion against the forces that tell me I should stop.

ALICIA ELLIOTT, *A Mind Spread Out on the Ground*

THE COMMUNAL REALM

is the color brown, to represent *aki*—dirt or earth. It is the time to honor our connection to the land and each other, and the time to plant seeds and make changes on the communal level. It is spring, the time of planting and waiting.

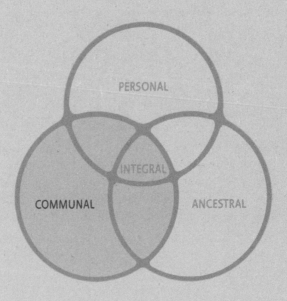

Maybe you don't know strength
until you've rested beneath
the branches of a magnolia tree,
feeling the weight of her regal, waxed leaves.
Maybe you don't know community
until you've watched ants
rebuild what was broken
by a world much bigger than theirs.
Maybe you don't know fortitude
until you've noticed geese
fly to the furthest border of warmth
to protect their children.
Maybe you don't know compassion
until you place your hands in the dirt
and feel the pulse of the earth,
her heart and soul welcoming you.
Maybe you don't know time
until you run your fingers
over a river rock,
their skin softened by generations of magic.
Maybe you don't know yourself
until the mirror of the water
reminds you of your goodness
and brings you home again.

6

CHILDCARE
AS RESISTANCE

I put a picture of my eight-year-old self on my computer desktop because I needed to look at her closely. A few months into trauma therapy, I recognized with the help of my therapist that I had been blaming my child self for the problems I encounter today in my body and experiences.

Essentially, I was blaming her for the trauma inflicted on me, trauma I had no choice over. I was expecting her to somehow be stronger than she was, until I realized that she was always strong, always finding new ways to protect herself—to protect *me*. The picture on my computer is of little me standing on a beach, with shoulder-length, light brown hair. I'm holding a shell out to the

---

Even though I write this chapter (and this book) as a parent, it is a chapter on the work of childcare for all of us, whether we are parents or not. We all have children in our lives, our communities, our families, and our systems—children who need love, care, and listening hearts. This chapter is about resisting through loving and listening to them as the wise beings that they are, remembering that care today is also care for the generations who come after us.

camera. I'm curious yet guarded; I'm adventurous yet unsure; and this has perhaps marked who I've been since then.

Learning to trust my body and my soul's strength again, learning to lean into the work of healing, requires that I let my child self know that she is amazing and worthy of love. She had to deal with so much more than she should have had to deal with, and she did everything she could to survive it. She is brave and strong and beautiful, and she has gotten me here today. The work of re-parenting myself has given me the courage to pay attention to the way I parent and care for the voices and stories of my own children.

My kids will of course know difficulties—I cannot give them a perfect or trauma-free life. But I can enter into embodiment with them. I can keep myself engaged and listening. I can think of my young self as I look at them and help them dream of a beautiful, glowing future. That is our work as adults, the work of caring for the children around us *and* the children in us. It is the work of resistance in a society that views kids as a nuisance or as creatures to be quieted, tamed, or controlled. Our children hold deep wisdom. They are the future in every way, and we should honor them as we learn to honor our child selves.

I am so appreciative of the people who are doing incredible work on decolonizing toxic parenting practices. For example, @latinxparenting on Instagram and Twitter has been an incredible source for those of us asking how we can raise our children with love, listening, and compassion, all while re-parenting ourselves with love and compassion along the way. In a recent Instagram post, they say about BIPOC (Black, Indigenous, and People of Color) parents: "We need new systems to replace old ones. We need to be fought for. We need rest and ease and play. We are not burdens, we are worthy and sacred humans raising worthy and sacred humans. Treat us as such."[1]

Our parenting practices today are very much connected to the inner children inside each of us, in how we respond to and repair our relationship with them. But we are in the Communal Realm now, and caring for the children around us is about more than just our personal preferences and choices. We know that care for children should extend beyond our own, and that our neighborhoods, communities, schools, and any entities that we engage with should be safe places for our children.

We don't have to look far to find evidence that we have used and punished children. Just look at the Trump administration's detention of thousands of immigrant children, some of whom died while in our supposed "care." That moment in United States history is not the first time that immigrant children have been treated poorly, but it is a moment in present history that should compel us to do whatever it takes to ensure that all children are safe and protected. Resistance requires it of us. In 2022, a number of states passed bills that target queer and transgender children and their caretakers—through policies and laws, our country's leaders are telling these children that they do not matter enough to be protected. When we refuse to care for _all_ our children in society, we are missing out on the work of solidarity and resistance—we are choosing the status quo instead of the steady, hard, beautiful work of healing and care.

Because I am married to a policing scholar and my children and I are Indigenous, difficult conversations come up often in our home. We talk about resistance; we discuss the fact that police still find ways to break up Indigenous religious ceremonies[2] or target Black and Brown men and boys, and that Indigenous women and other relatives go missing and their communities often don't have the resources to find them. There are many moments when I am flicking through the news reels in my own mind, having to decide which stories to tell and which to save for a later time. How much do I tell my Potawatomi children so that they understand the dangers they will always face in a nation that doesn't value who they are? Our future generations are going to be leading everything eventually, and preparing them for that future means

it's a hard balance

celebrating who they are, letting them be kids, and also telling them the truth.

In early 2022, Florida passed the Parental Rights in Education Act, also dubbed the "Don't Say Gay" bill. Its purpose was to keep educators from teaching about sexual orientation or gender until after a certain age, basically erasing the real identities and experiences of trans and queer students in schools. Understanding the harm this does—not only to our LGBTQ+ children but to *all kids* who aren't learning how to value and love one another—will have ripple effects for years to come. To love our inner child well, we must love *all* the kids in our communities well. But we know how cycles of oppression work—how our children are traumatized or abused and carry that into adulthood, sometimes healing, sometimes passing that trauma on. Do we recognize that the ways we treat our children, especially the most marginalized ones among us, has consequences either way? Are we willing to resist the systems we've created that limit the thriving of our kids?

i was never taught about this ←

Since June 2021, over a thousand unmarked graves and bodies have been discovered at various residential schools across Canada, with more following in the United States, and likely far more to come. This discovery was horrific, yet unsurprising for Indigenous and First Nations folks across Turtle Island; many of us are familiar with the history of residential schools, where children were taken after being forcibly removed from their homes and families to become "civilized" by Catholic teachers at these government and church-run schools.

The fact that this truth is so covered up in America's history books is a great source of violence to all Indigenous people, including our children. In Canada and the United States today, Indigenous children are still taken from their families and adopted into non-Native households, many of them evangelical Christian families, who are essentially doing the ongoing work of assimilation and colonization that those schools first aimed to do. What was once "kill the Indian, save the man" has now been cloaked in more socially acceptable language but has the same underpinnings of violence: "assimilate the child" and "save the child, save society." It is imperative that we understand this: it's no coincidence that the ones being taken are *children*, or that so many were taken out of their cultures at a young age, causing intergenerational trauma and harm with lasting consequences. For so long, we taught children to be silent at the dinner table, even as we knew, and still know, that they hold the future. As Anishinaabe people, we believe that children are sacred beings, capable of touching the Divine, of experiencing God on a level that we as adults do not understand. When we force our children to forsake who they are to enter into a colonized society, we commit a horrific form of harm that too often goes unnoticed.

Care for Indigenous children happens by all of society investing in our cultures and in our language programs, letting children see themselves represented on television and in other forms of media. It means paying attention to laws that force Indigenous children from their own homes and cultures. We must pay attention to both our history and the systems we have in place today to see where we go from here in caring for the children in our midst.

Cherokee reporter Rebecca Nagle shares about the Indian Child Welfare Act (ICWA) on her award-winning podcast *This Land*, following a few cases of Indigenous children being (often forcefully) adopted out of their families. To better understand the problems not just with these cases but with the foster and adoption systems in general, we have to know about the ICWA. Nagle explains in her series:

> ICWA is there to make sure Native kids get through foster care and adoption safely. First, it requires child welfare agencies to make active efforts to reunify the child with their parents. Second, the law allows tribes to advocate in cases that involve their

how can this be legal

71

children, or move the case to tribal court. And lastly, if a child can't be reunified with their parents, it sets out placement preferences for where that child should go next. The preferences go like this: first are members of the child's family, then members of their tribe, and then other Native homes.[3]

If we followed the guide of care that ICWA provides, Indigenous children would be safe and remain connected to their cultures and communities. But the world we live in deems those with privilege and power to be the ones who most often win in the end. What does this say about the Communal Realm that we have helped create? And how can we fix it, especially when Indigenous, Black, and Brown families are often trapped in cycles of poverty that make it that much easier for them to be targeted by these systems?

All children are valuable and deserve protection and love, which is why we need to understand history and today's societal norms—so that we can do a better job of protecting them. This is part of the work of resistance. Even as I write this, ICWA is being fought at the US Supreme Court level by states (and families) that are calling it unconstitutional.[4] As colonization continues to dictate the way we understand our society and cultures, our acts of resistance require that we approach care for our children from their personal homes to their communities and beyond. And when we cannot trust these broken systems to care for so many of our children, we fight to change them.

In *All about Love*, bell hooks writes about how to protect our (collective) children and how to decolonize our ways of parenting our children by both loving and respecting them. Ultimately, she says, "Love is as love does, and it is our responsibility to give children love."[5] A racialized, colonized, white-supremacist society is created not on a foundation of love but on a foundation of violence. We need to step back and ask how that can be both reimagined and re-created so that our children have opportunities

how would that be unconstitutional?

to create the futures they dream of and desperately need to make this world a better place.

I am not raising my children to be evangelical Christians.

At least not the kind of Christian I became as a child. I remember standing in my living room one day, looking out a window, wrestling with myself, because the Christian faith I was surrounded by told me that I was a disgusting sinner until I prayed a prayer that saved me. So there I was, wondering which parts of me were disgusting before age seven, when I prayed about Jesus coming into my heart. Which parts of me were not worthy of love by God when I was six years old, five years old, two years old? Which parts of me were deemed too lost to be redeemed, and which parts of me would forever be stained by those sins I had supposedly committed when I didn't even know what a sin was?

Our home doesn't have conversations about personal sins, nor do we talk much about conversion experiences or the fear of hell or reward of heaven. We practice the Seven Grandfather Teachings (based on ideas of humility, honesty, wisdom, bravery, truth, love, and respect), and we talk about kinship with the creatures of the earth and respect for others' religions and cultures. We take seriously the responsibility of living as communal people and showing up with our gifts when they are needed, and we work to ground ourselves in that wide, expansive love so we never forget that we belong to one another and to those around us. We make mistakes as parents, and we process through how to make amends, heal, and do better. It's a constant process of *becoming*.

In 2020, Interfaith Philadelphia launched its first youth program, called Walking the Walk, in which teenagers were given "experiences, skills and resources necessary to live in a diverse world."[6] Young people had access to other cultures, religions, and spiritual ideas, so that they were more equipped to value the lives of others as they prepared to enter the adult world. Our children

[handwritten margin note: I have been struggling w/ this]

are brilliant, wise, and nurturing, and if we don't ruin that for them, they have the chance to become the leaders of a new generation, one that is diverse in every way and has a better connection to the earth than we ever did. I hope we give them the tools they need to get there.

The Seven Generations (or Fires) Prophecy, an important and central piece of our Anishinaabe culture, tells of a time when the seventh generation will have to choose between knowing who we are and forsaking who we are. Will we honor Mother Earth or continue to abuse her? Will we resist the status quo of hate or live into it, perpetuating cycles of harm?

Resistance in the care of our children isn't just about raising them with the right moral or spiritual compass but is also about giving them the space to be curious about the world outside their front door, about how *Kche Mnedo*, Great Spirit, moves and breathes in all things. Care for our child selves, care for the children around us, is about embracing that curiosity and remembering that it is never too late to ask the silly questions that open wide our imaginations and help us dream of a better world.

This, too, is resistance.

A note to my kids:

When you were born, I thought to myself that I'd do everything possible to teach you resistance and help you understand the world.

Somehow, it turns out, you teach me how to resist and help me understand the world.

And so we are the enduring legacy of kinship with and for one another.

Every day, you remind me of the whys and the hows, and when I forget, you show me that loving the child in myself and others is one of the greatest gifts I can give.

When I forget, you show me that curiosity and humility are pathways to healing our relationship to the earth.

When I forget, you show me what love is and isn't.

When I forget, you show me how to be both fiercely passionate and gentle all at once.

When I forget, you embody resistance, and heal generations before you and after you, all at once.

You are our world, and we are because you show us how to be.

Thank you for being my teachers.

I love you always.
Mom

RESISTANCE COMMITMENT: Who are the kids and youth in your community? Take some time to ask them questions about the future: What are they excited about? What kind of world do they hope to help create as they get older? Remind them that who they are is important *now*, and that who they are becoming is a gift to all of us.

7

ETHICAL PRACTICES
AS RESISTANCE

Our spiritual realities do not exist in a vacuum.[1] Anything that happens to one happens to all; oppression and injustice affect all of us, on all levels. If we truly believe that our souls are connected, we also have to acknowledge that this will move into all areas of our lives—the way we practice solidarity, the way we live in our bodies, the way we embrace one another. So when we ask what ethical practices of resistance are, we are essentially asking *how* we do this work, and how it affects every aspect of who we are and how we live our lives in connection to one another.

Ethical resistance stems from much of my interfaith work, where I meet others from all walks of life who are asking questions about how we can share our world and our practices with one another without appropriating others' practices or silencing them, especially those who are from marginalized identities or communities. In many spaces, Indigenous practices and important parts of our cultures are appropriated by others, especially those

Capitalism seems to be at the root of a lot of problems

from dominant culture. When parts of a culture are westernized and commodified as "products" to be sold in our capitalist society, we are appropriating, not appreciating. How do we have this conversation? Where do we draw the line?

There are teachers who have been writing on these topics for a long time. Cherokee activist and professor Adrienne Keene explores this topic as it relates to Indigenous peoples on her website, Native Appropriations. Indian yoga practitioner Susanna Barkataki covers appropriation within yoga spaces in her new book (which we will discuss later in this chapter). There are teachers all around us who don't just answer the question *Is this appropriation?* but who also help us understand *why* it is and what we can do to stop it from happening again and again. Remember: we are in the Communal Realm, where our actions and, yes, even our intentions affect those around us.

Jewish scholar and interspiritual teacher Mirabai Starr approaches it like this: "We risk cultural appropriation whenever those of us from dominant cultures borrow the symbols and spiritual practices from colonized cultures without fully understanding their context or the depth of their cultural meaning."[2]

At its core, appropriation is an interaction where someone from dominant (often white) culture tells someone from a different culture—or acts in a way that conveys to the other person—that their way of practicing or understanding their own cultures/ stories/peoples isn't enough on its own; it must be westernized or stolen to really matter. It's why we get white yoga spaces and brands geared toward skinny bodies and namaste jokes. It's why we see "Pocahottie" costumes at Halloween or stores selling witch kits complete with white sage that hasn't been ethically harvested.

But understanding and working against appropriation is just one part of the practice of ethical resistance. Let's return to the larger questions: *How are we doing this work? How are we embodying resistance and denying the status quo of hate and oppression?* If you've gotten to this point in the book, then you are about the embodiment of resistance, and I am so grateful you are here. We will make mistakes. We will forget that we belong to one another, and then we will remember again, make amends, and move forward. This is all part of the process. *— important to remember*

Ethical resistance is about more than just making a decision to practice resistance; it's also about _how we practice it._ How is the work we do and the way we engage the earth and others grounded in support and solidarity for everyone?

Now might be a good time to revisit the introduction of this book, where we made these words our medicine: **I am a human being. I am always arriving.**

Even in this messy, complex, beautiful work of honoring one another, we remember our humanness, our stories, and we use them to guide us.

Because we live in a largely virtual world, many of our conversations and interactions happen on social media. This is a space where we can and should pay attention to our *ethics of resistance* by asking how we use these spaces well. We should always consider our responsibility and privilege—and should examine our practices on social media through this lens. Whose voices are we amplifying? How can we practice resisting ableism in our online spaces? Can our virtual world be a safe one for queer folks?

My use of social media is, above all else, focused on tools and resources for learning and the exploration of ideas, as I have shared in earlier chapters. Being in these spaces helps me ask questions. As I have gained more followers over the years, I've come to see that I have a certain responsibility to those who follow me. My words matter, just as my resistance matters. How do we steward our words and ideas well—*ethically* even? In our online conversations, how are we centering the narratives that disrupt the status quo? How are we listening to and pointing out the work of those on the margins, those that society and social media marketing teams deem a threat?

Going beyond this, what do practices of ethical resistance look like in our communities? We may have forgotten what this is like in the wake of COVID-19, but sharing a meal around a table is a beautiful form of resistance. Over the years, I've gathered with Muslim friends to eat together; I've made wild rice dishes for Thanksgiving dinners; I've shared a Shabbat table with my Jewish kin. And the dream of sharing a table with others continues to guide me forward in the work of resistance, because something as simple as eating together, celebrating who we are and where we've come from, keeps us going when things get hard.

Let's talk about yoga and wellness practices and how these can be a place to practice ethical resistance, both in person and on social media. I attended a yoga class a few years ago at the local gym in my neighborhood and left wondering if what I'd experienced had honored the yoga traditions we should be listening to and learning from. In the class, we didn't get any background on what yoga is or on the meanings of the terms used; we listened to a mixture of Native flute music and new age classical music, and the focus was on the wellness of the body instead of the harmony of the mind, body, and spirit. Many people have turned to yoga as a space of true healing and embodiment, and it has changed lives. I would never want to take that experience away from anyone, but I do want us to recognize how yoga is appropriated by white (including Christian) culture.

In her book *Embrace Yoga's Roots*, Indian yoga practitioner Susanna Barkataki helps us ask, "Why aren't some people, and some teachings, being listened to, uplifted and given platforms? Why is what we know as yoga in the West so watered down and so far from the roots a full practice offers?"[3] As Barkataki writes, yoga is about union, and when we infuse our yoga spaces with whiteness, it is an injustice, a disembodiment. She goes on to say that "when we interrupt appropriation, we are practicing *asteya*, or non-stealing."[4] So once we become aware of the appropriation in yoga spaces, what do we do to practice ethical resistance? We can start by reading books like Susanna's—invite your local yoga studio to read it with you. We can learn from and listen to marginalized voices that have been pushed out of Western yoga spaces, those like Tejal Yoga, a beautiful yoga studio I found on Instagram that focuses on "diverse representation for all people of color in yoga and offerings that are inclusive, accessible for all body types, income and experience levels."[5]

Tejal Yoga and other studios like them need folks to support their work by signing up for classes or supporting them on a monthly basis. Another teacher I've learned from is Aarti Inamdar, who offers yoga mentorships and other classes and services. Voices like those in the South Asian community and the queer community, and other marginalized voices, deserve to be centered. This is the tip of the iceberg when it comes to actions that are required for ethical resistance, but it is a start. We can begin where we are and go on the journey of unlearning toxic practices and learning healing ones. Again, the work of ethical resistance isn't just about attending a yoga class; it is also about asking *how* to deepen our knowledge of and respect for yoga's roots and how to resist the white, Western status quo that often commodifies and whitens spaces that are meant to be inclusive and holistic.

Conversations like these are a lesson in *bodies*—which bodies are considered worthy of our spaces, and which bodies we want teaching and leading us. As I stated earlier, yoga spaces, and many fitness and wellness spaces across the country, have become formatted to fit the skinny, white, female body, normalizing that particular body rather than all other body types that are perfect for yoga. Ethical resistance means paying attention to the many ways our institutions—medical, religious, fitness, social—tell fat bodies, transgender bodies, disabled bodies, short bodies, and Brown and Black bodies that they are not enough. When we begin to normalize the beauty of *all bodies*, we will gain more love for ourselves and for each other along the way, leaning into community, into resistance, into love.

As I've shared a few times, our practice of ethical resistance is tied to every part of who we are, including our very bodies and the systems created around them. Therefore, we must also consider stereotypes and myths that we perpetuate around one another's bodies, cultures, ethnicities, races, and religions. An episode in season 3 of the show *Madam Secretary* makes an important contribution to this conversation. Matt Mahoney (played by Geoffrey Arend) is the secretary of state's speechwriter. He is half Pakistani and a casually practicing Muslim, and in episode 6 of the season he is accused of supporting a terrorist who bombed a coffee shop in his hometown. Matt gives a powerful speech to his team, explaining that if a white man bombs a coffee shop, no one expects all white men to support that act. But when a Brown man who is perceived to be (or is) Muslim bombs a coffee shop, all Muslims must answer to society about whether they support this act.

It is a glaring and important critique, and we should take it seriously as we consider our resistance work. Even when we are fighting for change and paying attention to atrocities that happen all over the world, we must keep our stereotypes and biases in check, and we must recognize the benefit of the doubt that we constantly give to white activists, scholars, and leaders but not to immigrants, Indigenous people, Black people, or other people of color.

In 2022, the Body Love Uprising movement spread across the world, gathering women and all who identify as female to talk about and celebrate our bodies, to name what they've been through and move forward in solidarity together. V-Day is a global activist movement to end violence against all women, girls, and the planet.[6] I gathered online with faith leader Jacqui Lewis and V, who created this V-Day event, as we bore witness to each other's bodies and stories and pointed to the wisdom of Mother Earth. Essayist Terry Tempest Williams spoke of this liminal moment we find ourselves in, and as I think about this, I am convinced that the *ways we practice resistance must always be tied back to our relationship to the earth.*[7]

Because the earth matters, our bodies matter. On February 13, 2022, Christina Yuna Lee, a Korean American woman who was walking into what should have been the safety of her home, was killed. This was not a single incident but speaks to an increase in violence toward Asian people and especially Asian women. The NYPD reported a 361 percent increase in hate crimes toward Asian Americans since the year before,[8] and as COVID-19 restrictions lift, that number is likely to increase.[9] If our ethics are based on the standards we adopt and accept as a society, our status quo is hate—hate of Asian bodies, and in particular, hate of Asian women's bodies and violence toward them. So long as this hate continues, no one is truly free.

In *Native*, I wrote, "Indigenous bodies are bodies that remember."[10] So are Asian bodies, Black bodies, trans bodies, Sikh bodies, queer bodies, immigrant bodies, Latinx bodies, two-spirit disabled bodies, fat bodies, Jewish bodies, Buddhist bodies, men's bodies, women's bodies, nonbinary bodies, kids' bodies—*bodies remember.* So today, resistance is honoring the body, going back to that chapter on embodiment, rereading it, and coming back here to ask *how, ethically,* we care for one another's bodies. Maybe it begins with truth-telling, with naming, with the hard reality that violence is too often our guide.

How do we resist?

We hold space, with ourselves, Mother Earth, and one another. Here, in this Communal Realm, this realm of seed planting, the realm of waiting and trusting, we hold space. And as we do that, as we lean in and listen to one another's stories, maybe we build what ethical resistance is supposed to be. Maybe here we are sensitive enough, compassionate enough, to make room for more of the same. And when we mess up, we face it and do better.

It begins here, with our bodies.

It begins here, with our spirits.

It begins here, with each other.

And from here we can begin to dream ourselves toward a society that holds to a standard of solidarity and love. That's the world we build toward.

RESISTANCE COMMITMENT: Find a yoga studio to support on a monthly or yearly basis—one that prioritizes diversity in their yoga teachers and trainings, like Tejal Yoga. Begin conversations in your communities about how to prioritize marginalized voices in local fitness spaces, including yoga studios.

8

SOLIDARITY WORK AS RESISTANCE

Because I'm an author, I often get asked about the intended audience of my books. In one questionnaire, I answered this question by typing "human beings"—and then decided to be less snarky about it and list some specific groups of people. But the reality is, solidarity work really is about the work of *being human.* In our humanity, we are meant to love ourselves well, to love one another well, and to love the earth and the creatures around us well. Solidarity is grounded in the idea of belonging and kinship, so how can I possibly choose a portion of people in our society to read my book when I hope to learn from everyone and, in the process, have many learn from me? The reciprocity goes far beyond a target audience and marketing technique, and yet it's difficult sometimes to claim that we belong to one another when we have so badly abused and have harmed each other throughout the centuries. How do we practice belonging, share our work and medicine with one another, and trust that solidarity will truly happen?

Remember: we are still in the Communal Realm, the realm that is brown, representing *aki*—earth or dirt. It is our planting season, when we put seeds in the ground and see what grows from it. To me, that's exactly what solidarity is: a seed that begins inside of us. If we don't believe we truly belong to one another, why would we strive toward solidarity? The previous chapter's focus on the practices of ethical resistance laid the groundwork for us to ask in this chapter, If we don't know the *why* of our living resistance practices, how will we get to the place of solidarity?

Let's consider what solidarity is, where it comes from. The word originally came from Latin, meaning sturdy, firm, or undivided, and was later transformed into the French *solidaire*. Then, like many words, it found its way to the English language, where it now means "unity (as of a group or class) that produces or is based on community of interests, objectives, and standards."[1] Resistance is directly tied to embodying solidarity. To resist the status quo of hate, oppression, or injustice, we must be clear about what our solidarity is grounded in. What are the objectives and standards we are holding ourselves and each other to?

Solidarity movements matter; we have seen this throughout history. Solidarity comes at a cost, yet we gain so much when we gather together and commit to one another's well-being. When we refuse to look away from one another and instead choose to sit with one another's stories and proclaim that they matter, we are practicing solidarity. I practice solidarity with you when I remember that we belong to each other. Despite our best efforts to break free of one another, we are connected by our very humanity.

Take a moment to write down a few examples of solidarity that you've noticed throughout your life:

when my friends or family just sit and talk w/ each other and just share stories + ideas

In 2012, a few years after Travis and I moved from our hometown of Joplin, Missouri, to Fayetteville, Arkansas, we received a call asking us to come back to Joplin to participate in an event of solidarity and support for the Islamic community. On August 6, 2012, the Islamic Society of Joplin's mosque had been destroyed by a young man who is a self-proclaimed white supremacist. He set fire to the mosque, he said, because he "does not like the Islamic religion."[2]

We arrived in Joplin to a community of many exhausted Muslims and their allies, ready to do whatever it took to help eventually rebuild their community. We sat together in a restaurant conference room, eating and speaking quietly to one another. While we didn't really know what to say, we were committed to holding that sacred space together. We planned an outdoor event, where I played guitar and sang, Travis spoke to the crowd, leaders in the Islamic community shared, and many others brought words and music to remind our Muslim kin that they were not alone.

We know that violence toward the Muslim community is not new. Organizations like the Shoulder to Shoulder campaign were born out of this particular injustice and mobilize faith leaders to address anti-Muslim hate crimes and violence. They host free online seminars and equip people to actively practice solidarity with the Islamic community, and I am so grateful they are around to be a space where so many of us can learn and do better.

I've recently been learning about the difference between religious pluralism and interfaith organizing, thanks to the work of the Aspen Institute. These two ideas and embodiments are not at odds with each other; they are simply different frames or viewpoints from which to understand solidarity work. Religious pluralism, according to the Inclusive America Project, is "the state of being where every individual in a religiously diverse society has the rights, freedoms, and safety to worship, or not, according to their conscience."[3] What we practiced that night in Joplin was interfaith organizing, coming to a stage to say that our humanity brings us together and that when our kin are harmed, we are all harmed—that it matters and we must name it. Folks rallied and raised money so that the mosque could be restored. Resisting anti-Muslim hate brought us together. And because we live in a society that allows white, Christian supremacy to exist and perpetrate harm against minoritized religious communities, we must continue coming together, choosing to resist hate again and again.

This work isn't just about what we have in common; it's quite the opposite. If we want to be kin to one another, we listen to each other's stories, we honor how they are varied, and we celebrate those differences. Solidarity work doesn't happen only because you reflect who I am and are therefore worthy of my support. Solidarity work happens when we choose to truly *see* one another with all our similarities and differences intertwined. My hope is that in the future these interfaith and interspiritual spaces become less centered around the Christian American narrative and begin to take a shape that reflects the dynamic beauty of the religious and spiritual cultures all around us.

One of my greatest frustrations with the white, toxic evangelicalism we've seen in America, the evangelicalism that I grew up with, is that the creation of a cultural identity based in shame and fear of the "other" took precedence over accepting and celebrating other people as the humans they are. In her book *Jesus and John Wayne*, which traces evangelical Christianity's history in this nation, Kristin Kobes Du Mez writes about how evangelical marketplaces began, dating as far back as the 1970s: "The evangelical consumer marketplace was by then a force to be reckoned with, but this expansive media network functioned less as a traditional soul-saving enterprise and more as a means by which evangelicals created and maintained their own identity—an identity rooted in 'family values' and infused with a sense of cultural embattlement."[4]

We were taught that a simple two-minute prayer could somehow fix everything about one's life because it promised a future in heaven. And the bubble of our faith kept us held by fear and by beliefs that we were sure had to be truth. But that's not solidarity. That's not dialogue. It is colonization—taking the cultures, beliefs, identities, and humanity of another person or people and telling them these are not good enough.

One small way we approach decolonization in our solidarity work is to recognize and name the systems that perpetrate colonialism. Decolonization and solidarity work are both approaches that lead us *toward* one another instead of away, standing together rather than at a distance that lets us more easily name someone as "other." When we practice interfaith organizing grounded in ideas and tenets of religious pluralism, we begin the work of truth-telling, honoring one another's stories, and gathering together for the sake of all of us. We begin embodying *communal living resistance.*

We cannot talk about solidarity work as resistance without talking about the pervasiveness of police violence that has always existed. Indigenous people all over the world know the reality of this, as do immigrants; Black and Brown folks, queer and trans folks, and anyone who doesn't fit the mold of what is deemed a "good citizen." Frank Edwards, Hedwig Lee, and Michael Esposito document the risks of being killed by police based on age, race, ethnicity, and sex, and they found that young Black men face the highest risk of being killed by police. For women, the highest rates of death by police are among those in the Black and American Indian/Alaska Native communities.[5] While some see police as those who provide safety and order, others know police to be "agents of repression ensuring the survival of political elites and maintaining the political status quo."[6]

For too long, the conversation has been about "a few bad apples" or how "good" people can exist and participate in corrupt institutions. My father was an officer for the Bureau of Indian Affairs, which I write about in *Native.* The complexities of this are not lost on me. But it's because of the complexity that we have to be dedicated to the conversation, or else those on the margins will continue to be killed by police to protect the status quo built by white supremacy, greed, colonization, and hate.

In April 2021, as Derek Chauvin was being tried for the murder of George Floyd, a young Black man named Daunte Wright was murdered in the same city of Minneapolis during a traffic stop because of the air fresheners hanging in his front window. As we continue to see this pattern in the United States and beg for justice, it continues to play out across the world. In June 2021, Indigenous peoples in Brazil, along with their allies, protested Bill PL 490, which would take away their rights to their traditional lands. As citizens gathered in Brazil's capital city to protest, police met them with excessive force at the direction of the government.[7] These kinds of interactions happen all over the world, day after day. Practicing solidarity with those on the margins who are using their bodies to protect the land is an act of resistance against our systems and against the institutions that devalue the land and those who care for it.

In January 2022, the *New York Times* published an op-ed by an Anglican priest who called on churches to drop their online services during the ongoing pandemic to return to "embodied" in-person worship.[8] The backlash was swift, and readers demanded that the *Times* give space to disabled spirituality authors (preferably Black) instead. I responded by tweeting, "I really hoped that this pandemic would have us (especially church-going Christians) thinking about ways to expand gatherings to include disabled/immunocompromised folks & others on the margins—in fact, we are still spinning in our individualism, colonialism, and ableism."[9] When articles like this are written, or everyday societal decisions are made that neglect disabled and immunocompromised folks, the able-bodied among us are reminded of how far we have to go, and the disabled among us remind us that it's been this way for a very long time. This wasn't the first article written on this

hate

topic—throughout the pandemic, we witnessed different Christian leaders (yes, even *progressive* ones) calling for us to get back to "normal" in our churches at the expense of the immunocompromised among us.

In fact, religious spaces have been some of the most abusive toward disabled folks, and stepping into our resistance through solidarity is to name these truths and fight against them. Feminist author and activist June Eric-Udorie writes about her experience at a church when she was younger, when a man told her that taking Communion would heal her body of nystagmus. She writes of the hate aimed at her throughout her life, and of the moment she came to recognize the sacredness of her own body and experiences. After a journey of self-love and acceptance, she said, "I come to church happy in the body I exist in; I come to church knowing that I am not a mistake waiting to be fixed."[10]

One Sunday close to a decade ago, I brought my father to the evangelical church we'd been attending. Walking in with his cane at his side, he was immediately intercepted by a well-meaning young man who was part of the prayer team and wanted to heal my father of whatever ailed him. While finding our seats, we watched the young man and my father as they walked slowly up and down the side aisle, the young man intently praying for my father as he touched his arm.

My father was too kind to tell him to stop, so finally my partner intervened and brought him to our seats, but the entire service we were furious and embarrassed. My father, in his body, in his experiences, was not enough as he is to exist in that church without someone letting him know it the moment he walked in the door. And judging from the teachings of many in the church today, we still hold on to our benevolent ableism in the form of unsolicited prayers of healing and the laying on of hands when people never asked for it in the first place.

If anything, COVID-19 should have made it more clear that the world has left disabled and immunocompromised people be-

church = judgement for me different

hind again and again, denying them their humanity and refusing to make spaces safe for them. We witnessed the denial of those rights in anti-masking rallies and calls for an end to all online gatherings. As Black, queer, disabled activist Alicia Crosby tweeted, "The Church/US American Christianity steadily fails chronically ill & disabled folk. It's wild to see an entity hyperfocused on flesh get respect & care for bodies so wrong."[11]

When we create institutions and gatherings fit for only white, able-bodied people, we do not experience the fullness of the sacred. When we listen only to white, disabled voices, we also miss the complexity and intersectionality of other disabled and immunocompromised voices who need to speak to their experiences. The real question is, What will it take for able-bodied people to get angry enough to practice real solidarity with disabled folks, and when will we fight for change in institutions that have proclaimed some bodies wanted and others unworthy?

In her book *On Repentance and Repair: Making Amends in an Unapologetic World*, Rabbi Danya Ruttenberg writes,

> The work of calling our institutions to do better is messy, and it's not linear. Some institutions will be more courageous, will do repentance work with more integrity, naturally, because it's the right thing to do—but in many cases, this process will be long and fraught, and improvements in one area may or may not lead to improvements in others. We must constantly urge the organizations and institutions in our lives along the path of repentance, to show them that the way forward can be an ongoing process of more transparency, more accountability, more amends, more taking ownership, more structural change, more focus on care for those who were harmed and those who are most impacted.[12]

So what does solidarity with disabled and immunocompromised folks look like today? In a COVID-19-ravaged world, which is what we will be living in for a while, it looks like paying attention to mask mandates and following them in order to keep

some people are so unwilling to do anything for other people

others safe. It looks like making those decisions not just for yourself <u>but for others</u>, as surges in cases have meant hospitalizations for some. It's listening to disabled voices online and in real life, and it's paying attention to the ableism that we ourselves embody as able-bodied people. It looks like paying attention to conferences and events that don't make things accessible for everyone and speaking up about it. It means paying attention to ableist language and supporting disabled folks by reading their books and celebrating their work.

Solidarity means choosing not to look away from one another but instead leaning into each other's stories because they matter. We don't care about one another because it's another box to be ticked off for the diversity list; we care for one another because we are *kin*. That is resistance.

RESISTANCE COMMITMENT: Dive deep into your online spaces, your bookshelves, and the gatherings or institutions you're part of. How are disabled people treated? How can you speak to that? If you are disabled or immunocompromised, how can you find rest today, and who might you mute or block along the way?

9

PROTECTING THE LAND AS RESISTANCE

I want to come back to the idea of radical self-love and self-care as resistance and help us build on it here in the Communal Realm. Self-love is about coming home to ourselves and healing ourselves. But it's also about reconnecting (or perhaps connecting for the first time) to the land, to the work of kinship, and in turn, to the work of communal healing—which means that caring for the lands and waters around us is living directly into resistance too. *humans are meant to be communal*

I often imagine that when I practice care for myself, a circle of light emanates from the center of my being, connecting me to somebody else. The light is constantly flowing, constantly connecting us to one another, so that when I care for myself, those around me receive something, and when those around me care for themselves, I receive something too. Somehow, self-love and self-care become reciprocal with those around us. Another way to imagine it is that every time you care for and heal yourself, a ripple emerges out of your being and reaches somebody else and encourages them to heal and care for themselves.

Mother Earth, or Segmekwe, is always doing this for us. She is our teacher, emanating light and teaching us how to do the same. As I wrote in the chapter on embodiment, one of the greatest tools of colonialism is to disconnect us from the land and, in doing so, to disconnect us from our bodies and communities. So the work of protecting the land is for everyone, is reciprocal, and is exactly what we are made for.

As we dive into this chapter, I want to make something clear: It is not the job or role of *only Indigenous people* to care for the land. If you are a human being and you are reading this book, you have a relationship to Earth, whether you recognize it or not. You have a relationship to Segmekwe, and there is much healing that can and should be practiced in this relationship. Maybe it's been a while since you've spoken with her; maybe you're repairing certain aspects of your relationship; maybe you don't even know where to begin. Protecting the land as an act of resistance begins with the realization and acceptance that we belong to her, and Indigenous folks across the globe are leading the way in this work.

So much of the way we understand land in America comes down to colonization and religion. Before this nation was officially founded, European Christians were given permission (in the name of God) to take the land that they wanted and get rid of the people who got in their way. From the beginning of their time here, they saw the land as an investment, as a commodity, which automatically severed the sacred relationship to Mother Earth. Do you want to better understand climate change? Look to colonization. Do you want to better understand Christianity as we know it in America? Look to the history of colonization in the church, and pay attention to how uncomfortable many Christians get when asked to pay attention to the land, to honor her as a teacher.

Because we were virtual so much in 2020 and 2021, I had a chance to lead several interactive workshops with various groups and organizations across the country. One of my favorite activities is leading people to write a love letter to Mother Earth—or, as I say sometimes, a *define the relationship* letter. One step toward decolonizing is to begin resisting the idea that the land is a commodity or product. When we step back and deconstruct the ideas we were taught growing up—in particular the idea that we are meant to have "dominion" over the land and basically do whatever we want to Earth—we begin to crack open our souls to the reality that we have an extremely sacred relationship to our Mother.

Climate activist, writer, and podcaster Mary Annaïse Heglar leads fierce and courageous conversations on climate change and how we got here. She has tweeted that "'humans' caused climate change much in the same way 'humans' caused slavery or colonialism or poverty or war or hunger or . . . you get the point."[1] She has also written that "the fossil fuel industry was literally built on the backs and over the graves of Indigenous people around the globe, as they were forced off their land and either slaughtered or subjugated—from the Arab world to Africa, from Asia to the Americas."[2]

We cannot talk about protecting the land and our relationship to the earth without talking about colonialism and the legacy of white supremacy in America. In *Native*, I write about the Doctrine of Discovery, but for those who need a recap, Pueblo descendant Sarah Augustine spells it out in her book *The Land Is Not Empty*: "The Doctrine of Discovery is a theological, philosophical, and legal framework dating to the fifteenth century that gave Christian governments legal and moral right to invade and seize Indigenous lands and dominate Indigenous peoples."[3]

You cannot understand our relationship to the land, here or around the world, without understanding the ways colonialism has dominated and attempted to destroy Indigenous people's connection to the land. But for this to truly matter, it has to be *history does not account for everyone*

talked about and learned, and the history we've been given must be
unlearned. I have been in groups of activists where hardly anyone
knew what the Doctrine of Discovery was, even though we know
that placing ourselves in this moment in history, especially as
Americans, requires that we reckon with how we got here—and
that includes how the land became a product to be sold instead of
a being to be revered and respected. It's discouraging to feel like
we have to start at the beginning, a beginning we've never even
reckoned with as a nation. But that's what we've got to do; the
land deserves our hard work and a deep willingness to reorient
ourselves toward the truth.

Let's remember, though, that the struggle to protect the land
isn't happening only in the United States. Across the world, where
colonialism has spread its tendrils into the gentle soil, the land has
both resisted and been subject to pain and hurt. In India, Indigenous farmers have been trying to protect their seeds and the land
from companies like Monsanto for generations through various
laws and collective action. Vandana Shiva, Indian scholar and environmental activist, writes about the fight to protect biodiversity
in India: "Indigenous knowledge systems existing in medicine,
agriculture, and amongst fishers are the primary base for meet-
ing the food and health needs of the majority of our people. . . .
Where commercial interests are concerned, biodiversity itself has
no value; it is merely 'raw material' for the production of commodi-
ties, for the 'mining of genes' and for the maximization of profits."[4]

In the push for commercial production over biodiversity, farmers and Indigenous healers have been taken advantage of, used,
and killed for the sake of profit. This is the way of colonization,
and it is why we *must* resist it. When we sever the ties our bodies and souls have to the land, as we have done again and again,
we lose ourselves, we lose each other, and it becomes so difficult
to find our way home again.

Sometimes I think of the climate emergency as Mother Earth screaming that she's done. I wrote about resilience above, as a facet of self-love and self-care. Here, as we consider our relationship with Earth, the scenario is this: we are the oppressor, telling Earth again and again that she is beautiful and resilient while we pillage and take from her, while we push her back down and tell her to keep getting up. She has been resilient again and again. She has resisted again and again, and yet here we are, fighting not just for the survival of humanity but for her healing. Fighting climate change isn't just so that we can be comfortable again—a people-centered climate argument isn't really a climate argument at all. Fighting climate change is about giving Mother Earth the love and respect she has always deserved.

Dr. Wangari Maathai is a Kenyan scholar and environmental activist who created the Green Belt Movement. In a speech to the World Congress of Agroforestry, she says, "Here in Kenya we have been involved in long term campaigns to urge farmers and government alike to respect and protect, conserve and restore biodiversity in forests so that we can benefit from environmental services they provide."[5] Once again, we are pointed toward the importance of protecting biodiversity all over the world and entrusting the Indigenous peoples of all lands to care for the resources we benefit from as humans, and to teach us to do the same.

If we want to talk about resistance, how can we not talk about all of our structural injustices being connected? Indian farmers struggle to protect their land, just like the people of Brazil, just like the women of Kenya, just like Indigenous folks who gathered in Minnesota to protest the Enbridge Line 3 pipeline, all of them fighting against police, governments, and corporations. In *All We Can Save*, a book of essays on the climate crisis, editors Ayana Elizabeth Johnson and Katharine K. Wilkinson write in the introduction: "The same patriarchal power structure that oppresses and exploits girls, women and nonbinary people (and constricts and contorts boys and men) also wreaks destruction on the natural world. Dominance, supremacy, violence, extraction, egotism, greed, ruthless competition—these hallmarks of patriarchy fuel the climate crisis just as surely as they do inequality, colluding with racism along the way."[6]

Given that these patriarchal power structures have brought so many of the problems we have today, we have to be careful about the movement we continue to build. Ojibwe activist and climate lawyer Tara Houska has concerns about the way we build these movements, which can easily become mirror images of the very institutions and designs we are fighting against. If our climate movements are about money and not about the land herself, we have missed it. She writes, "Corporations spend millions on campaigns to sow distrust and hatred toward anyone who disrupts the status quo. . . . I wonder what would happen if the environmental movement truly stood with the land it speaks of, side by side with impacted communities who bear the brunt of the climate crisis."[7]

She later writes, "I do not believe we will solar panel or vote our way out of this crisis without also radically reframing our connection with our Mother."[8] This is why I tell people to write letters to Segmekwe. This is why we cannot approach the climate conversation from a static, data-driven reality only—we have to invest our bodies and souls in this.

Resistance against the status quo of conquest, of hate, of pillage, means reconnecting our souls to the land that holds us. I want to share with you one of my favorite poems from Mirabai Starr's lovely book *Wild Mercy*. The poem is below, and as you read about the Great Mama, I want you to think of her as Mother Earth, Segmekwe. Imagine Mother Earth gathering you to her lap. After reflecting on Mirabai's poem for months, I wrote a response to it—a response from the Great Mother, in this case, from our Great Mother, Earth. I hope you can sit with the poem and my response as you lean into your Resistance Commitment, as you ask what it might mean for you, for all of us, to reconnect with the lands and waters around us.

Here. Come here. Take a moment to set aside that list you've been writing in fluorescent ink. The list that converts tasks into emergencies. Items like "feed the orchids" become "If I don't accomplish this by 11:00 a.m. tomorrow morning the rain forests are going to dry up and it will be all my fault." Or "If I fail to renew my automobile insurance I will probably crash my car and everyone will die." Or "This friend just had her breast biopsied and that friend's brother-in-law beat up her sister and my aunt just lost her job with the symphony and my nephew is contemplating divorce and I must call them all, and listen to them for an hour each, and dispense redemptive advice."

Gather your burdens in a basket in your heart. Set them at the feet of the Mother. Say, "Take this, Great Mama, because I cannot carry all this shit for another minute." And then crawl into her broad lap and nestle against her ample bosom and take a nap. When you wake, the basket will still be there, but half its contents will be gone, and the other half will have resumed their ordinary shapes and sizes, no longer masquerading as catastrophic, epic, chronic, and toxic. The Mother will clear things out and tidy up. She will take your compulsions and transmute them. But only if you freely offer them to her.[9]

The Great Mother Responds

I gathered you up yesterday. You were tired, worried, your mind full of everything and nothing. You were living an apocalypse, anxieties rising with the second, so I handed you a basket. I handed you an oxygen mask too, and we took deep breaths together until eventually your heartbeat slowed. You were sleepy, finally, like a child who has thrown a tantrum long enough, who has let it all out and suddenly aches for closed eyelids and comforting dreams. So I picked you up and held you, sang to you while you fell asleep.

When you woke, everything was still everything, but you—you were different. You calmed, and carried on with the tools to continue the calm, even when things began to unravel. You took your inner world and proclaimed it to be good, sacred even. You trusted the deep breaths, and as you slowly emptied your basket of worries, you looked back at me, questioning. You looked back at me, holding the to-dos in your right hand and the oxygen mask in your left, and as you'd learned, you took a deep breath and journeyed back to your life. I'll see you tomorrow, though, and the days after, every day that you need me. I'll be here to hold you, to remind you of the oxygen mask and the basket, to remind you that my waiting lap is ready and that my arms are warm. I am always here when the inner world gets shaky. I am always here to unburden you.

RESISTANCE COMMITMENT: Begin a "Letters to Mother Earth" journaling practice. When you have space, sit still with pen and paper (or laptop/audio recorder) and send letters to Mother Earth. Begin to heal your relationship, to define it, to dream of what healing might come in the future as you connect with her.

10

KINSHIP AS RESISTANCE

I knew that a large swath of progressive Christians weren't ready to have real conversations around kinship when Twitter blew up over a ceremony, organized by Union Theological Seminary, in which students gathered to apologize to plants. After having Potawatomi author Robin Wall Kimmerer visit campus, Union faculty and students decided to hold a service in honor of their plant relatives. Folks brought houseplants and other potted plants into a room and spent time in prayer, mourning, and conversation.

Christians mocked them online, angry that a seminary would hold a service for plants. They suggested that the students were worshiping the plants and not God; they were furious and confused, scoffing at those who would dare try to have an active relationship with a houseplant. I was angry. I temporarily changed my Twitter name to "Kaitlin Curtice Probably a Pagan," reasoning that if progressive people cannot understand what kinship is, they won't see my humanity for what it is either. If they don't understand the sacred in a houseplant, they won't understand the sacred anywhere.

There is a long-standing history of demonizing those who have a relationship to the land. Look to the Salem witch trials of the 1600s, where women who communed with nature and the land were considered evil and murdered for it. Look to missionary conquests all over the world that villainize other cultures for using plant medicines. Look to how we have treated Indigenous peoples throughout history, how we have been considered "savage" and "uncivilized" for not accepting the god of the white man. Look to the way Christianity has "othered" so many cultures and peoples for recognizing the sacredness in Mother Earth and our creature kin.

I knew that despite all the tweets in support of Black and Indigenous voices and all the retweeted booklists and all the hired talks, much of the progressive Christian world didn't actually create or sustain inner change. I knew that the white American church still believes that our creature kin are less than us and that those who have a kinship-based relationship with our creature relatives are pagans and animists (which in itself isn't a negative way of being in the world, but it is demonized by institutional Christianity).

But kinship is for everyone; we can all have a constantly healing relationship to this earth, ourselves, and one another. Choctaw elder and Episcopal priest Steven Charleston writes about kinship in his book *Ladder to the Light*: "Kinship must be maintained. It must be constantly recognized, affirmed, and renewed. Therefore, balance must be maintained. The equilibrium of diversity must be upheld through justice; therefore mutual respect must be practiced."[1]

So how are we maintaining kinship? How are we responding to Mother Earth as we live in this Communal Realm, when she tells us she is tired of the way she's been treated? How do we respond to others who are trying to lead us toward a better relationship with Earth and each other?

❦

There are other ways we are missing the work of kinship in the book-publishing and public-speaking worlds. For the first few years of my writing career, I often entered Christian spaces where I was treated as the "first"—the "first" Indigenous woman to write about colonialism in the church, the "first" who wasn't a man, the "first" who wasn't evangelical. I know, of course, that I'm far from the first and have often reminded audiences of that, but in the span of years in which I was writing, right after Standing Rock and during the Trump administration, I entered a world of difficult conversations on what the church has done in the past and what its responsibility is in the future.

In other words, it was lonely. I was lonely. Before I realized it, I was a faith leader trying to navigate my own identity, and people love to chat about identity, especially on podcasts and in question-and-answer spaces after talks. I began to realize how uncomfortable I was in many of those spaces, but I couldn't figure out why—I didn't have the language to name it as traumatizing and triggering until Indigenous women and other women of color confirmed my anxieties.

What is "just a chat" to many podcasters or church audiences is often an experience with colonization, microaggressions, and trauma for many of us who come from marginalized communities. But we internalized years of gaslighting, so much so that we began to believe that we are being too sensitive, and we tell ourselves they've paid good money for us to speak to them—or they haven't, and we're supposed to be grateful for the "exposure."

Today, I know I am not alone, and I hold conversations with other women who are battling colonial mindsets everywhere. Kinship to us is holding this space with each other, acknowledging that the worst part of all of this is that we think we are alone in it until we realize we are not.

For years I said that I'm just not good at deflecting and thinking on my feet. I thought that if I didn't like doing podcasts, it was because I needed more practice. But I learned that underlying these

this is such a pivotal moment

encounters is actually constant, ongoing colonization that puts us at risk of being traumatized over and over again. At the risk of further harming ourselves, we stay quiet, or we keep engaging these conversations to give the impression that we enjoy them.

Until.

Until we find out we aren't alone. Until another woman reaches out to say, "That happened to me too." And then we know that none of this is worth our pain and traumatization.

So we begin setting boundaries.

We begin saying no.

We begin choosing ourselves and the safety of community that won't gaslight us or make us feel like we overreacted.

I began to share my stories, and I found others who were struggling with their own boundaries. Many were new authors who were Black, Indigenous, queer, disabled, and women of color, wondering how to navigate these spaces when so much expectation is put on us to sell our books to colonial societies.

I love you, but you keep hurting me is the refrain that describes so many people's relationship to the church in America today. Queer people, trans people, disabled folks, those who journey with mental health, Indigenous people, Black people, Asian folks, those who grieve too much, immigrants, Latinx folks, all of those on the margins, all who overlap across these identities, all who are different from the whitewashed, white-formed status quo. We have said again and again, *I love you, but you keep hurting me,* and at some point, either you leave the abuser or you spend your entire life staying and hoping they'll change.

We are in a time in which we need to name the abuse, we need to challenge the abuser, and we need to step away, and many of us have. While I am so grateful for friends who are challenging the status quo and resisting white supremacy from within the church (and other) institutions, there are those of us who no longer at-

I have been / struggling w/ this

tend church, no longer belong to the denominations that once felt like some sort of home for us. <u>Our act of living resistance is wandering and asking if we can create community outside the hate that exists within the walls of the white American church.</u>

My friend and Anishinaabe author Patty Krawec wrote a beautiful book on the work and ideas of kinship. She writes powerfully about this relationship to ourselves and each other:

> For Indigenous peoples, kinship is not simply a matter of being like a brother or sister to somebody. It carries specific responsibilities depending on the kind of relationship we agree upon. An aunt has different responsibilities than a brother. If we are going to be kin, then we must accept that these relationships come with responsibility. In our settler-colonial context, relationships between us are built on a paternalistic foundation: charity and good works, helping the less fortunate. Those who are part of the society that created the problem become the ones who think they can solve it. So, we must move from recognizing the *fact* of our relationship to actually existing together, in *reciprocal* relationships.[2]

Kinship definition

Kinship can feel like a very abstract thing, but imagine it like this: I have a string attached to my body, to my heart center, and it goes directly from my heart to yours, and to every other living creature on this planet, to Mother Earth herself. Whatever I do with this heart, with this body, affects you; it travels across that thread and finds its way to you. And whatever you do or embody travels to me, to the ants, to Grandmother Moon, to someone across the world we've never met.

We do not get to escape each other, no matter how colonized or traumatized we may be. This is kinship. As I shared earlier about boundaries, it's important to note here that <u>kinship is *not* a pass to stay connected to abusers or toxic people.</u> Our dream of a more interwoven world, I hope, will heal many of those relationships as we set healthy boundaries and imagine what kinship has to teach us.

Kinship is rooted in storytelling. It is grounded in the act of listening, of taking in one another's stories, which is something we have failed at miserably in many ways. The fear of listening to another person's story is that we can't make them a this-or-that human being. The reality is, when we lean in and really experience another person's story, we can begin to sort out the *why* of the situation—*why* they are wounded by this, *why* they are acting that way. It doesn't make behavior okay, but it's important for us, in the light of kinship, to remember that we are all complex beings with nuanced stories, that we all come from complicated relationships that have shaped us.

Brené Brown, in her book *Braving the Wilderness*, shares about the importance of entering into each other's wilderness, each other's stories: "We're going to have to learn how to listen, have hard conversations, look for joy, share pain, and be more curious than defensive, all while seeking moments of togetherness."[3] Humans have always been complicated, our stories varied but also, somehow, the same. Going back to the importance of having healthy boundaries, I am not suggesting, nor is Brown, that we put ourselves in toxic and emotionally harmful situations just for the sake of taking in another person's story. We are beyond that in many ways. But, just as kinship works, we cannot deny that we belong to one another on some level, that love calls us toward each other, and that transformation is possible.

The firefly, or *wawatesi* in Potawatomi, is one of the most magical creatures in the world. Fireflies use their glowing lights to communicate with each other in the summer months when it gets warm enough for us to swim in the rivers and listen to the frogs sing at night. But they are elusive—to see them, you have to gaze into the darkness and wait, with patience, for those little lights to appear. And no matter how old you are, you cannot stop the rising excitement in your chest, the childlike magic that takes over—the firefly, the lightning bug, is there, lighting up, and you get to experience it because you believed the wait would be worth it.

I believe kinship works in the same way. *Kinship* can be defined simply as *close relationship* or as *a sharing of origins*. And sharing of origins—relationship—that takes time too. It takes waiting in the silence, in the dark, in the quiet spaces, for trust and companionship to blossom. It takes communicating with one another along the way to make our communities and healing networks successful.

Our relationship to Mother Earth should be based on ideas of kinship, that we belong to one another, that our love is reciprocal, as Robin Wall Kimmerer so beautifully writes about in *Braiding Sweetgrass*. We should, at some point in our lives, decide that the journey of kinship is worth the waiting to understand what it means to belong to another—to Mother Earth, to the creatures around us, to the people in our lives, to all our relatives.

And I am not just talking about our blood relatives when we talk about kinship. As many of us have learned, a blood connection is not always enough, and is not always safe. Many queer and transgender youth can tell you this, those who have been pushed from their own homes and deemed unworthy of a religion built on white supremacy and colonialism. They know full well what it means to have *chosen family*, as many of us do. Kinship is about that chosen relationship, the origins of who we are as sacred and beloved beings all across this earth.

Even our relationship with the Divine, *Mamogosnan*, Creator, the Great Spirit, God—this is based on kinship, on shared origin, on ideas of what it means to be loved and to love. When I was little, I used to ask God how they were doing. I thought that caring for the entire world, the galaxies around us, must be so exhausting, with so many painful stories to hold—so I'd pray, *How are you doing with all of this?* I never really got an answer, but the answer wasn't necessarily the point. I asked because I wanted *kinship*.

The ironic thing is that for as long as I went to church, people would pass by one another, their smiles plastered on for a few hours each Sunday morning, asking, *How are you?* We would answer one another, *Oh, good! How are you?* as we made our way to the worship service. That empty, hollow space eventually made me furious every time I entered, wondering if I could really tell these people how I was doing. I wondered if I could say how angry I was that ICE was in our city or that our political leaders had no sense of urgency to care for the land that we live on. Could I tell them that I was grieving the death of a friend or that God felt far away and stained by the colonialism I felt throughout Christian spaces? No. I don't believe I could have. And while that's not every church environment, it's enough of them to convince me that in the white American church, we aren't patiently working toward kinship. We aren't willing to wait in the uncomfortable spaces, to quietly stare into the dark until we see a light calling out to us.

But I hold on to that sense of wondering how the Divine is doing. I felt it when I visited the beach with my family on our first family vacation. Watching the waves of the Atlantic Ocean pound against the shoreline, our voices were quieted by the urgency, the noise. Those same waters carried the *Mayflower* to those shores, the people who would cause devastation to so many Indigenous peoples on this land. Those sacred waters have so many stories to tell in the rush and the wind, in the tide rolling in and out and back in again. I wonder how the water is doing, and I wish I could know. So I keep listening. I keep watching. I keep waiting for kinship to take hold and teach me what it means to be a human being in relationship. And when I journey across Mother Earth, whether I'm in a bustling city or the excellent quiet of a deserted place, I remember what kinship is, what relationship is, what community is, and I am grateful for the chance to learn more.

RESISTANCE COMMITMENT: Kinship is a deep, reciprocal relationship. Hold a gathering, ceremony, or service of some sort where animals, plants, and people are present or represented. Read poems, pray, and have conversations about what kinship means and how you can better practice it as a community.

PART 3

THE ANCESTRAL REALM

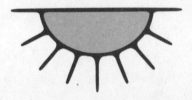

Life isn't always that tidy. Many of us find ourselves, at various points, a victim, a villain, and a champion.

JULIE RODGERS, *Outlove*

THE ANCESTRAL REALM

is blue. Blue represents *mbish* (water), fluidity, movement, and the space we inhabit as we interact with our ancestors. Resistance is fluid, moving work. It is the season of summer, when we notice what grows and blooms for future generations, what comes out of the hard work of planting that we did in the Communal Realm.

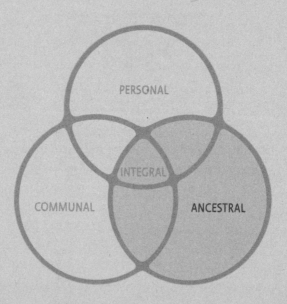

I want to tell you something.
That ache, that exhausted longing,
that hole that seems to fill with nothing but air—
Remember the nothingness that fills it.
One day, you'll need space to breathe,
to remember,
to accept,
to grieve,
and that big open space inside you will
become home.
It is a space that is ancient and modern,
there and here,
everything upon everything,
nestled in the quiet.
And one day, you'll need it.
One day, you'll go there
and you'll stay a while,
and all that air around you
will be the very thing
that cocoons you
and prepares you again
for the outside world.
I want you to tell me something.
Do you feel it?
Do you long for home?
Do you need that air?
Do you believe in it?
Do you believe in you?

11

DECOLONIZING AS RESISTANCE

We all have ancestors. No matter who we are, those who came before us have brought us here, to this moment, to this life, and we interact with them on a daily basis, whether we realize it or not. In Indigenous cultures all over the world, there are various ways to honor our ancestors, whether it's through spirit plates to honor them with food, an altar in our home that constantly reminds us of their presence, or simple daily interactions with prayers and lit candles.

I believe healing can happen after those we have loved and known have passed on, and I dearly hope that when I pass on, healing is still possible for me through those who come after me. We believe in the Seven Generations in our Potawatomi culture, which means we believe that the things we do today will affect those seven generations after us. And in the same way, seven generations before us, our ancestors believed the same thing when they were journeying this earth.

I have ancestors from various places, with various histories, and I reckon with that on a daily basis through my own actions and embodiments on this earth (if you want to read more about my story, you can find it in my last book, *Native*). I owe something not only to my ancestors but to everyone around me, as an active participant in living history. I owe myself, my ancestors, and others the risk of living a good life that is marked by decolonization, care, and solidarity.

The Ancestral Realm is an ethereal but also a very real place where we interact with our ancestors, where we acknowledge them in our very bodies even as we acknowledge that they have passed on. The Ancestral Realm is a perfect place to practice decolonization, to name the ways in which our ancestors did what they could but didn't do enough; the ways our ancestors still had so much to accomplish but didn't have the space, resources, or time to do it all; the ways our ancestors rely on us to change the things they couldn't or didn't change.

Stop for a moment and consider your ancestors. Maybe you don't know them, and when you try to picture them, their faces are a blur. Even so, take a moment to acknowledge them. While reading Resmaa Menakem's book *My Grandmother's Hands*, I came to a point where he asks the reader to close our eyes and practice imagining our ancestors. I will admit, I feared the worst—that I wouldn't picture anyone, just a vast empty space on the inside of my eyelids where I was waiting for something magical to happen.

But then they came. I saw a large group of people, holding hands, walking down a long dirt path past me. And as they passed, the woman on the end closest to me reached her hand out, beckoning me to join them. They were ancestors from all parts of my family, on all sides, coming together in some sort of healing journey that I could not fully understand, and they were graciously inviting me into it. I accepted. I took the woman's hand, and we walked on together, all of us, acknowledging the work I still have to do here before I pass on and become the ancestor too. After that meditation, the way I understood my own ancestors changed because I'd been invited to be an active part of not just my own healing but theirs as well.

The Ancestral Realm is where we meet with our ancestors and name what hurts. It is where we pay attention to what kinds of ancestors we want to be one day. It is where we grow and find healing, acknowledging that healing goes on within us and beyond us all at the same time. The Ancestral Realm is where the magic happens.

Decolonizing work begins inside us—as individuals and as a whole, inside our institutions and frameworks, our offices and places of worship. Decolonization is heavy work and should never be taken lightly, but the struggle is very much in the everyday, in the work of speaking truth—even when the next-door neighbor supports a man full of hate and prejudice. The truth is that this work is hard as hell, yet it is always an invitation, a question that asks, *Is there a better way?* As author adrienne maree brown writes, "Our radical imagination is a tool for decolonization, for reclaiming our right to shape our lived reality."[1]

In autumn of 2021, I spent some time at an Airbnb in a rural Pennsylvania town. As I sat by the firepit in the backyard, I thought: the land didn't choose to be split up for profit; the horses next door didn't choose to be domesticated; the fire that burns in the firepit didn't choose to be contained, and so *what choices are ours to make?* What, in our everyday life, can we shift, transform, or reimagine to become something different, something headed toward that better way? Where have we come from, and where are we going, and how are we paying attention to the world around us along the way?

Before we go further, I want to name what I named at the beginning of this book, which is the danger of terms becoming fads. *Activism* and *resistance* are meant to be embodied, and so is *decolonization.* And yet we've seen people claim the work of decolonization when it is anything but. I've witnessed groups of white folks boast about how they'll teach others to decolonize without collaborating with or learning from any Indigenous people. This is dangerous, and it is ongoing colonization. If we want to take decolonization seriously, then let's consider it as the real, radical resistance that it is.

I can't write about decolonization without writing about the church's role in the colonization of so many peoples throughout history, especially Western, white Christianity's role as we have come to know it in the United States. Many of us who have survived on the margins of the church or society know that colonialism has deep roots, as does patriarchy. While reading Kristin Kobes Du Mez's book *Jesus and John Wayne*, I was reminded of this reality—of America's obsession with the Wild West, with the fierce and violent masculinity of the frontier and thus Christian men, and how it has affected so many of us on the deepest levels.

As a young person, I once attended a church camp called Armor. The entire camp was themed around a militaristic idea of Christianity, calling us to "put on the armor of God," as we read in the New Testament. Through camps like this one and the overall nature of the evangelical churches I was raised in, I had adopted a nationalistic view of God and of my Christian responsibility, as well as the message that as a woman my place is in the home, supporting whomever my future husband would be. I was obsessed with Rebecca Saint James's songs "Wait for Me" and "Go and Sin No More," which I would often listen to before I left for school in the mornings as a charge to share my faith with others and to remain abstinent until marriage. Without knowing it, I had adopted colonial, militaristic, patriarchal views of God, and for me as a woman, these views translated into people-pleasing and a fear of authority.

But colonization is bigger than a toxic church camp. The systems and institutions built by acts of colonization have been

not just big things

created and sustained at every level, macro and micro. They come from the most personal spaces of our own families and dinner tables, and from the largest corporations and most seemingly liberal of our democratic leaders.

In *Native* I wrote, "Decolonization doesn't mean we go back to the beginning, but it means we fix what is broken now, for future generations."[2] Decolonization helps us ask questions about the systems, mindsets, and spaces we grew up in. But here, I want to go beyond that, because truly living into resistance means coming to terms with the reality of colonization and being brave enough to ask what that better way forward really is.

According to the book *Pulling Together: A Guide for Front-Line Staff, Student Services, and Advisors*, decolonization is the process of deconstructing colonial ideologies of the superiority and privilege of Western thought and approaches. It "involves valuing and revitalizing Indigenous knowledge and approaches and weeding out settler biases or assumptions that have impacted Indigenous ways of being. For non-Indigenous people, decolonization is the process of examining your beliefs about Indigenous Peoples and culture by learning about yourself in relationship to the communities where you live and the people with whom you interact."[3]

In late 2020, farmers in India began a mass protest, calling the world to see the injustice of recently created Indian laws that would deregulate the sale of crops, resulting in catastrophe to small, local farms.[4] Sikh scholar Simran Jeet Singh shared about the importance of paying attention to what was happening in India, since it barely made any US headlines. In a *Time* article about the movement of Punjabi Sikhs to resist the government in order to have better support of agriculture, Singh writes that the oppression of India's farmers isn't just about what's happening with India; it also speaks to the dangers of unjust and oppressive governments and institutions all over the world.[5] In this moment, as it has always been, protest as an act of resistance is important to us as human beings seeking to belong to one another.

Let's pause for a moment to name something that decolonization *isn't*. Many of us have seen white activism and white feminism cloaked as decolonization and justice actually used as a tool of harm toward marginalized leaders and populations. While white activists are deemed "peaceful protestors," activists who are Black, Indigenous, queer, minorities, or other people of color are considered "violent." In the same spaces, white activists will be lauded for their work and marginalized activists will be villainized. White feminism will often ignore the work of Indigenous and Black feminist movements that connect us back to the land, back to ourselves. Feminism that's merely performative won't bring healing or call us to actually begin the work of decolonization. And even though these conversations are difficult, white leaders *must* listen to marginalized folks advocating not just for their communities but for humanity, for Mother Earth, for one another. And white leaders must support their work along the way. These movements are meant to be communal, connected, flourishing, and that means whiteness cannot be at the center as it has been throughout history. Something must change if we want to fully live into resistance.

When we learn about and embody decolonization, we are looking to those who lead us to show us what it means and *why we must resist*. Farmers in India, protesting to protect the land, folks all over the world fighting to dismantle oppressive systems—these people show us how to demand a better world. The power of protest has helped people hold governments and institutions accountable for the decisions they make.

There is a valid distinction between decolonization and indigenization, and different folks have argued for both. In short, decolonizing is what we've been describing: bringing awareness and working to dismantle colonization in and around us. Indigenization takes this one step further, requiring that non-Indigenous people see the leadership of Indigenous people as valid, valuable, and necessary to build a better world going forward while not forgetting how we got here in the first place. Some argue that focusing on decolonization puts too much emphasis on the colonizer, while indigenization puts Indigenous peoples at the center. According to the Indigenous Corporate Training organization, "Both decolonization and indigenization require the cooperation of Indigenous and non-Indigenous people, governments, organizations and institutions."[6]

When our decolonization work is void of Indigenous voices, we are missing the point. Indigenous peoples all over the world lead the fight for the earth, for connection, and for kinship. To "decolonize" without understanding what colonization has done and how important it is to listen to Indigenous people keeps us from dreaming of or beginning to create the world we've been waiting for.

While we are here in the Ancestral Realm considering decolonization, let's jump right into Thanksgiving, something I am asked about year after year. Families and classrooms ask me to lead them through what they can do to decolonize the Thanksgiving table. It is so powerful to be grateful. In reality, we should be holding gratitude every single day, paying attention to the world around us, to the sacred, with the knowledge that we are held and loved. To indigenize this holiday is to learn that we should be grateful every day.

For those who intend to celebrate Thanksgiving, I offer, as a starting point with hopes you'll continue to grow and learn, three ways to decolonize *and indigenize* the holiday.

First, tell the truth. An online Potawatomi archive puts it like this:

President Abraham Lincoln officially established the holiday as a way to improve relations between northern and southern states as well as the U.S. and tribal nations. Just a year prior, a mass execution took place of Dakota tribal members. Corrupt federal agents kept the Dakota-Sioux from receiving food and provisions. Finally at the brink of death from starvation, members of the tribe fought back, resulting in the Dakota War of 1862. In the end, President Lincoln ordered 38 Dakota men to die from hanging, and he felt that Thanksgiving offered an opportunity to bridge the hard feelings amongst Natives and the federal government.[7]

Indeed, this holiday is built on lies—not just the lies of how Europeans treated the Wampanoag people when they arrived here but the lies buried by the government along the way. The most powerful thing we can do is get rid of the myth while still holding the sacredness of our time together. Start by telling the truth, and even consider holding this day as a day of mourning in solidarity with Indigenous folks.

Next, celebrate Indigenous foods and cultures. Buy books by Indigenous authors to read from during your time with family and friends, and order cookbooks like *The New Native Kitchen*, getting ingredients from Indigenous protectors of the land or Afro-Indigenous farmers who are tending land across the country. Supporting these organizations and Indigenous creatives is entering into the work of unlearning and paying attention, which I hope leads us deeper into conversations around and embodiments of decolonization and indigenization.

Third, make a plan. The difficult thing about the month of November is that it is both Native American Heritage month and Thanksgiving, so it all gets rolled into one. I wrote about this in *Native*. It's an exhausting month for me (and for many Indigenous folks), and the healthiest thing I can usually do for myself is to go inward a bit, care for my family, and hope that the world is learning to honor us as they go. One way to honor us is to make a plan for the coming year (without directly messaging Indigenous folks for information). Start in November and map out ways you can learn about Indigenous cultures by telling the truth *and* celebrating who we are throughout the year.

Begin with your home first, with the land you currently dwell on. Start there, learning about the peoples of the land, both past

[handwritten margin note: like the real after / a funeral]

and present. Make tangible commitments to learn more, and learn alongside others. It shouldn't be about shame. It is not our fault that we didn't learn how to honor Indigenous peoples in our school curriculums or society growing up. But once we know, we cannot unknow, so use the time as an exciting space of solidarity and decolonization, and challenge institutions around you to do better by Indigenous peoples.

Read books, listen to podcasts, order wild rice from organizations like Honor the Earth and make a dish to serve to your closest friends. Patterns become habits, and habits can change the way we understand ourselves and the world around us.

Decolonization and indigenization are partners, and when I think of you all reading this book, you become my partners too. We link arms and pray for a better world together, and as we do so, we step into what that work requires of us. Eventually, that better world will show up because we were willing to practice resistance together.

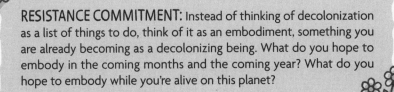

RESISTANCE COMMITMENT: Instead of thinking of decolonization as a list of things to do, think of it as an embodiment, something you are already becoming as a decolonizing being. What do you hope to embody in the coming months and the coming year? What do you hope to embody while you're alive on this planet?

12

GENEROSITY AS RESISTANCE

Generosity is a form of resistance in the world that connects to our sense of belonging and to the work of storytelling. It has its place within the Ancestral Realm because this way of being in the world has ripple effects outside our particular circle, and even our particular lifetime.

Generosity is based on the idea (and embodiment) of giving *more* than is necessary of your time, your energy, and sometimes even your money. With generosity, you go against the I-can't-say-no culture by *not* giving up all of yourself and disappearing under the expectations or orders of others. Generosity is not toxic codependence or silencing ourselves for the sake of others. It is something else entirely, a way you expand into the world to fulfill your own gifting for yourself and those around you.

When we lived in Atlanta, we attended an event on Emory's campus put on by the Tibetan Buddhist monks from the nearby

Drepung Loseling Monastery. They spent days preparing a sand mandala, and then the following Saturday, a group of us showed up with our children as the monks shared with us the significance of the mandala and we witnessed the methodical, tender destruction of the piece.

After it was over, the monks invited the children forward, and each was given a bag of sand. The children were instructed to take home the sand and to practice blessing and prayer with it, sprinkling the sand wherever they wanted goodness and love to follow. A few days later, I was writing at my desk when my youngest child, about five years old at the time, snuck up behind me and sprinkled sand over my head. On other occasions, at night, he would take a pinch of sand and sprinkle it over the floor, praying. He was practicing the gift that was given to him by these monks, and he has never forgotten what it means to make the choice to bless someone else instead of cursing them, to use his inner world as a space of generosity, just as they taught him. We need more generosity like this in the world.

If you've picked up this book, chances are that you are guided by some spiritual practice or set of beliefs that are important to you. You understand that resisting hate in the world requires that we draw from a deep and sacred well as humans. We recognize that resisting hate means living generously in any way that we can. I have always believed that it is important for me to name that the work I do, and who I actually am as a person, is to be both fierce and gentle, to speak the truth but to do it in a way that invites others into that truth and into the sacred work of storytelling. For my own journey, it has been important to name that, to be generous with the liminality of who I am.

Consider for a moment who you are at your core, who you want to be in this world. Beyond work or family, beyond social circles or the boxes you check online, *who are you at the deep center of yourself? What do you embody in this lifetime?*

Write or process your thoughts here:

Generous living means that we engage all of those around us every day, in a nonlinear way. We understand that there are seasons to life, that there are generations, and that there are cycles of life happening all the time that we can pause to recognize. Sometimes living generously means knowing that future generations will inherit what we give them. How can we best prepare them for the resistance they will need to embody in their lifetime? If you have ever heard of the potlatch ceremony or other similar ceremonies, you know that gift-giving and generosity are important to many Indigenous cultures across the world. The Kwakwaka'wakw people of British Columbia continue the tradition of the potlatch today, believing that "a rich and powerful person is someone who gives the most away."[1] This ceremony (and truly their everyday existence) is marked by celebration and generosity, and we have so much to learn from it.

In a society where we value scarcity mindset over generosity, how can we rewire what we believe about power and status? What if we really understood that the more we have, the bigger the responsibility to bless others? What if today's millionaires and billionaires, today's corporate executives, truly understood this? How would it change everything about America's inequities?

To better understand how we cultivate and keep generosity as a form of resistance, we first have to consider the economy of fear that is all around us, and the fearful tendencies that we have internally developed, whether we recognize them or not.

Fear holds great power. Some of us know this because we grew up in spiritual environments that used fear as a mechanism for finding or pleasing God. I remember being on a mission trip to Colorado, where our group was hosting a Vacation Bible School at a church. One night after the group devotional time, I was caught in what felt like a near panic attack in the stairwell, thoughts and fears swimming in my mind about the reality that my best friend at the time was going to hell unless I saved her. Her soul's destination after death was somehow completely my responsibility, and I had been failing.

I carried responsibilities and fears like that throughout my childhood. We were taught in our Baptist churches that we were the insiders and that the rest of the people in the world were outsiders; it was our job to save souls and welcome people into some sort of reality that God had always wanted. Looking back now, I know that this is all an ongoing, vicious form of colonization and abuse that has plagued the earth for centuries.

My modal response to life was fear—fear that I wasn't doing enough, fear that someone I loved would die before they were saved, fear at the thought of walking up to strangers to tell them about God, fear that I was sinning even more than I thought I was, fear of a vengeful God who would eventually destroy the world and take only a chosen few to paradise.

These were religious fears, but they bled into all other parts of my life. I had nightmares for years and was terrified of the dark; I held my fears in my body and developed digestion issues as a child. Fear was the constant hum beneath the surface of my life, and I had no idea how to control it or process it with safe listeners.

And what happens when so many of us grow up with that hum of fear, always vibrating? Unless we later go on to face it, name it, and heal from it, economies of fear will emerge. When I finally realized that maybe atheists aren't that scary and other cultures around the world (including my own Indigenous culture, which I'd learned to villainize as well) have beautiful truths to teach us all, the hum of fear began to fade away. When we are raised in an economy of fear, our response is to "other" one another. It is part of the reason we practice and embody anti-Blackness in our society today, and even in our Indigenous communities against Afro-Indigenous folks. We have somehow taken in a message of scarcity, and it has scared the hell out of us, and in turn, we've hurt one another. Kinship and belonging are paths toward healing this.

When God, Mystery, and the Sacred began to expand in and around me, the hum faded, and in its place was the expanse for a new kind of generosity to form—for gifts to show up. I often imagine that if the "good Christian men" who "founded" this nation had arrived without that fearful scarcity mentality, things might be different. If they'd encountered Indigenous peoples from a place of curious kindness and understanding instead of this need to dominate in the name of a vengeful god, history might have unfolded differently.

Resisting the economy of fear is directly tied to learning the truth about the history that has unfolded around us, the history taught in our schools and churches, the stories we tell. If we don't draw a picture of America as this nation of the great first Thanksgiving, what will it become, and who are we really? The idea of deconstructing and asking difficult questions about our family's past, about our country's past, fills people with such dread that they would rather create banned-book lists for entire school communities than approach the truth with care, nuance, and understanding. As my dear friend Gareth Higgins writes in his book on fear, "We're often afraid of the wrong things, or we fear the right things the wrong way. We find it difficult or impossible to tell the difference between the story in our head and what we're actually facing."[2] But we must be brave enough to face the stories and to face the truth. This is why storytelling is so important but can also be incredibly dangerous! What stories are we telling? What are they rooted in? And how can we begin to find healing in stories that have caused harm?

Afro-Indigenous author Kyle T. Mays addresses the importance of Afro-Indigenous peoples' voices being heard in the process of this truth-telling: "For people like me, there is little representation with respect to Black and Indigenous peoples. We often have to choose one identity or the other, depending on the circumstance. That is unfair, even tragic. Our histories are important, deserve to be told, in a parallel and systematic way."[3] Resisting the economy of fear means telling the truth, allowing yourself to grieve that the truth is not what you thought it was, and letting the work of healing replace that fear. When this process begins to unfold, generosity happens, systems begin to change, and whole communities are transformed by the process of truth-telling. In a way, we show up to one another with freedom to express our gifts in a more decolonized way that blesses those around us and brings ancestral healing to the forefront of our lives.

When my kids were about five and seven, I started singing to them at night, mostly my favorite jazz songs to begin with. "Just the Way You Look Tonight" and "Fly Me to the Moon" quickly became favorites. The latter, written by Bart Howard and famously performed by Frank Sinatra, is a love song, but it echoes a refrain that has existed throughout history, saying in essence, "Let's escape, let's go! Together, hand in hand, let's create a new way."

Reading Jenny Odell's *How to Do Nothing* reminded me of this constant human phenomenon of longing to leave the city, the busyness, and escape to the land, to the quiet. While it's worked for some people, and their lives have been drastically changed by that escape, often made possible by their privilege, many of us have had spurts and starts of escape, of "flying to the moon," and have returned to do the work set before us.

There can be danger to the idea of escape, of course. Billionaires Jeff Bezos of Amazon and Richard Branson of the Virgin Group in the United Kingdom want to create a new economy of commercial space travel, while many of us shout from earth the words of Buffy Sainte-Marie: "Me, I don't wanna go to the moon, I'm gonna leave that moon alone!" Escaping to colonize the moon while neglecting those who need help on earth wouldn't be an escape at all, and so we ask what it means to be present without giving in totally to the exhaustion around us.

Our family started a new nighttime tradition recently of meditations, a few minutes to sink down into the bed, to take some deep breaths and to focus on something good and kind. The meditations started with imagining our safe space, something that I often do when I am anxious at night. *Close your eyes and imagine a safe place where you are totally yourself and where you don't worry about anything. What do you notice? Who is there? What are you doing? Are you eating? Do you smell anything? Are you outside or inside? Let your imagination go wherever it needs to.*

One night, we did an exercise focused on music. We listened to the song "Uranus" from the album *Space* by Sleeping at Last. I pictured a busy city street with cars, and as the cars drove into the distance, they disappeared into a field of yellow flowers. As they disappeared, a large yellow butterfly emerged out of the field where the car was and rose up to the blue sky—*transformation, freedom.*

Another evening, I asked my kids what they would do to change something in the world to help people. My oldest wondered out loud what would happen if we got rid of money, how it would change our society—suddenly, he imagined, people would get what they need because there would be no hierarchy. We'd share and reimagine society. He was present to the dream of a new reality. He went to sleep that night with that dream, with that presence.

Mari Copeny, better known as Little Miss Flint, is a fourteen-year-old who brought attention to the clean water crisis, not only in her hometown of Flint, Michigan, but all over the country. Since she was eight, she has been using generosity as resistance, using her gifts to fuel incredible acts of kindness and care for others. Besides raising money for water filters, she also uses her voice to raise awareness and funds to gather backpacks for kids who need school supplies, as well as fundraisers for Christmas and Easter gift bags for children, among other projects. When our young ones tap into their power of generosity, something beautiful and deeply powerful happens: the adults start to pay attention, just like President Obama did when Mari raised awareness about what was happening in Flint.

When our souls align with our power, and when we push fear of scarcity aside, generosity happens, and the world changes. Along the way, perhaps healing is available for our ancestors and those who come after us are given a better starting place.

RESISTANCE COMMITMENT: Think of a time when someone was generous toward you. Maybe through their time, money, or other gifts, they shared something sacred with you. How did it change you? How are you tapping into generosity and leaving fear behind in your own life? How can you displace fear and share generosity with someone else?

13

INTERGENERATIONAL HEALING AS RESISTANCE

We hear a lot these days about intergenerational trauma, a phenomenon in which the descendants of a person (or peoples) who have experienced a terrifying event show adverse emotional and behavioral reactions to the event, similar to those of the person himself or herself. Intergenerational trauma is complex; it has many layers. Maybe this trauma was passed down from something that happened to one person in a family, or maybe it's more historical and communal—various traumas passed throughout history. An important example of intergenerational trauma is the damage done by Indian boarding schools and the silence and shame that so many Indigenous people have carried since their ancestors were forced into those schools or the very real trauma that descendants of Holocaust survivors suffer to this day.

We feel that kind of trauma in our bones, in our lives, the effects of generations of our ancestors' abuse and oppression. It manifests in different ways for different people, but it's there.

And it's important to acknowledge it as we strive toward resistance together, especially in this Ancestral Realm where we are acknowledging and reckoning with our own ancestors.

As one of my favorite authors, Dr. Clarissa Pinkola Estés, writes, "I urge you, ask you, gentle you, to please not spend your spirit dry by bewailing these difficult times. Especially do not lose hope. Most particularly because, the fact is—we were made for these times."[1]

Indigenous peoples all over the world, and many others, recognize the importance of this moment. While we live in a time that feels heavy, scary, and hopeless, let's recognize that it is also a time of social and spiritual uprising. We are living the Seven Generations Prophecy right now. The youth of our day are given a choice—colonization or the ways of their ancestors—just as we are all given this choice. As Indigenous people, we are at a critical moment, trying to preserve our languages and cultures, continuing to fight against corrupt and colonial governments and societies.

But I don't want to focus only on our trauma. As someone who writes on colonization and white supremacy on a daily basis, I want to find other ways to engage with the world and society. I need good medicine that will help keep me grounded and steady for the journey ahead. As much as we need to be informed about the intergenerational trauma we carry, I want us to focus on the intergenerational healing we carry too.

Related to the idea of intergenerational trauma is the concept of intergenerational resilience. The Alliance for Intergenerational Resilience (AIR), founded by researcher and educator Dr. Lewis Williams, is a worldwide organization that focuses on reconnecting to the earth as a way of healing intergenerational trauma and leaning into our resistance. Elsewhere in this book, I have written about resilience, honoring our ancestors, and healing our connection to the earth. But I want to go even deeper in this chapter, to pause a moment and pull it all together. To find and embody intergenerational healing, it is imperative that we go on a journey of healing our relationship to Mother Earth.

We are holding on, and as we do, I believe that resilience is building. From the AIR website: "When we gather together to work on the land, or to celebrate, or to tell stories round the fire— all age-old ways of being that connect us to our ancestry—we are suddenly able to remember what is important in our lives. By reviving our most timeless practices we remember what it is to be human. This we can use as a basis to imagine our future."[2]

Maybe as you're reading this book you feel like I'm talking about our connection to Mother Earth a lot, throughout each realm, throughout different cycles and seasons of our life. I want to make this very clear: repairing our relationship to the land and the waters, *no matter who we are*, is an essential part of living resistance and affects every part of our inner and outer world and life.

This is why intergenerational resilience is so much about connecting back to the land and healing that connection. We are all dealing with some sort of trauma in our lives, whether it's personal or collective. Honoring and naming that provides a path toward healing. In Toronto, near Humber College, The Willows is a program that helps kids connect to water and land. An article about the program explains, "Nature is not just seen as resource or commodity, but something that engages mind, body, heart and spirit together."[3]

These children are being taught and reminded that the waters have memories and stories, that the land holds them and all of their creature kin. They are gaining a foundation of decolonization from their elders. This is living resistance, seeking healing and finding it with Mother Earth.

Have you ever considered yourself a descendant of Grandmother Moon or Grandfather Sun? Do you consider them your elders and hope to learn from them, sit with them, and listen? Take a look at the cover of this book, designed by artist Alanah Jewell of the Oneida Nation. Notice the sun and the moon, the way they are part of the cycle of all things, the way they lead us through our cycles, seasons, and realms. They are our teachers. Have you considered the rivers and the rocks as teachers and elders? Have you spent time beneath a pine tree, recognizing that history has unfolded for generations in those shady spots?

Take a few moments to process this in the space below:

> I always feel the most connected + at peace when I sit alone, in silence in nature + w/ trees or talking w/ my family by a fire.

Intergenerational healing and resilience cannot happen unless we recognize our connection to the earth and work to heal it. Iain MacKinnon, Arianna Waller, and Lewis Williams write, "Many of us have become denaturalized from a sense of belonging to, and caring for, a particular place on Earth as part of an ancient human presence there, and . . . , relatedly, we have been made subject to a mode for living that contributes to ripping up the protective natural fabrics of our planetary home."[4]

If anything ties us both to our ancestors and to those who come after us, it's the way we care for Mother Earth and one another. Putting care into this relationship can actually heal us from generation to generation. It begins with the recognition that there has been a fracture, with naming the systems that have caused the fracture, and then telling the truth and beginning the work of healing.

My friend Tanya Tarr is a behavioral scientist who wrote a wonderful article at the beginning of 2022 on what it takes to start a new habit. As we consider healing and resilience, I'd like to apply her work to the way we understand our relationship to Mother Earth. Tarr writes that building new habits requires both learning and performance. We cannot get to the performance part of a new habit without taking time to learn it: "When we are in the learning phase, we are trying to develop how to automatically respond without consciously making a decision."[5]

What if the work of seeing our place in the world and focusing on our relationship to Mother Earth is also about forming a habit? If this is true, then we spend time (a lot of time) building our base of learning. We read. We write letters to Mother Earth. We process. We learn from Indigenous communities all over the world who have practices in place for connection and healing. We deconstruct and unlearn the colonial ideas we grew up with. We take in and take in and take in, and eventually the performance part begins to happen, and a more fully connected space on this earth is just part of our lives. Decolonization just becomes part of our lives, what we do. We live in more equitable and just ways because it's the habit we've formed. It all becomes part of who we are, a true embodiment of the work.

Many communities cultivate relationship with the land through sustainable farming. Afro-Indigenous farming communities are caring for land all over Turtle Island. The first time I stumbled onto one such place, Soul Fire Farm, I felt a swell of hope in my chest. When things feel heavy, I desperately look around for something to remind me that we still care about community and belonging and haven't forgotten that we are kin. I ordered a bundle of garlic from this farm while living in Vermont, and I cherished every clove because I knew the ancestral care that went into growing it.

Soul Fire Farm explains their mission this way: "With deep reverence for the land and wisdom of our ancestors, we work to reclaim our collective right to belong to the earth and to have agency in the food system. We bring diverse communities together on this healing land to share skills on sustainable agriculture, natural building, spiritual activism, health, and environmental justice. We are training the next generation of activist-farmers and strengthening the movements for food sovereignty and community self-determination."[6] This is living resistance. This is intergenerational healing and resilience happening in real time. I encourage you to order some food from an Afro-Indigenous farm and lean into how that connection to the land might heal all of us.

In the way that we are learning to repair our relationship to Mother Earth and the land, many of us as Indigenous people are learning to repair a relationship to those who came before us by learning our languages. I wrote in *Native* about beginning to learn Potawatomi, about that first moment hearing a Potawatomi prayer coming through my laptop speakers. It changed me, and it continues to change me. When I am overwhelmed by the toxicity or heaviness of the world, I return to our languages, and I am always cared for. In learning the very words my ancestors spoke, I am awakening something in my world today.

When my youngest child comes home from school and says, "Today I said *migwetch* [thank you] to someone at school when they handed me something!" I know we are healing. I know we are going to be okay. I recognize that we may not be fluent Potawatomi speakers at the end of our lives, but I also recognize the gift I have in learning our stories, our words, our embodiments in this world and this land.

The Ancestral Realm is the color blue, representing water and movement, the space where we shift and change, we become, we learn and unlearn, we grow, we stagnate, we grow again, all without shame or fear. Taking a deep breath, we say: **I am a human being. I am always arriving.**

And then we choose when, where, and how to arrive, just in this moment, just for today, knowing it connects us to those who came before and those who come after. To remember is a gift on this journey. It is a gift to see what grows, inch by inch, from the journey of our living resistance.

RESISTANCE COMMITMENT: Draw (or imagine) a large, horizontal oval on a piece of paper. At the left end of the oval, write "ancestors." In the middle, write "me." And at the far right end, write "future generations." Examine the way you exist in the never-ending cycle of those who came before and those who come after. Inside the oval, write, draw, or envision the things you hope for in your lifetime and in the lifetimes of those who come after you.

14

LIMINALITY
AS RESISTANCE

As we dive into this chapter in the Ancestral Realm, I am well aware that many of you may not be familiar with liminality. So let's start by breaking it down a little bit.

Liminality, to put it simply, is the psychological process of transitioning across boundaries and borders. In a time when we love to keep ourselves separated from one another with our ideologies, beliefs, religions, ethics, identities, politics, and so much more, liminality asks how we exist in those in-between spaces. So much of my own writing has embodied liminal space, and I've found that there are many others who are doing the same.

I have begun describing my life as existing in the liminal spaces where healing, grief, identity, spirituality, joy, anxiety, rest, anger, and so many other things meet. I also exist in the liminal spaces where I am doing healing work that reaches my ancestors who have passed on and all those who come after—I rest in this in-between space called life. This means that whatever resistance I embody, however I dream and imagine the world to come, <u>I do it because I believe that those who came before brought me to this moment and those who come after will take us beyond it.</u>

For a moment, let's imagine this realm that we are in right now, the Ancestral Realm. The magic of our existence is that we can remember our ancestors and learn from them, and at the same time, we can understand that we are, right now, ancestors in the making. We are looking to future generations who will one day remember us, remember what we did or didn't do and what kind of life we lived. The Ancestral Realm is blue, representing fluidity and movement, which is exactly what liminality represents too.

I began the Liminality Journal in fall 2021 as a place to share original poetry and essays about what it means not just to live in liminal spaces but to learn how to embrace them. In a dualistic world and society, liminal space, gray space, and even the beauty of queerness as it challenges the status quo are difficult for many. They require accepting a level of nuance and complexity into our lives and each other's stories that we are not always prepared for. But when we do, we gain a fuller sense of our humanity.

One of the projects on the Liminality Journal is a series interacting with blog posts that I wrote before I became a published author. My early days of writing were on my blog, which I called *Stories*. The posts were reflections on my life as a new mother, as a Christian, as a human. Many of the stories—basically journal entries that give insight into my first few years as a mother—are altogether too personal to ever share publicly. But those blog posts gave me a sense of purpose and helped me process all the ways I was asking what it means to be human in that space. Interacting with these old blogs posts as I am today is an act of resistance in and of itself, not to shame my younger self for the things she did not understand, but to pull her through to where I am today, and to integrate all of who I am *now*. It's about healing and invitation.

Liminality is a difficult thing to make concrete most of the time. I have an example from my childhood that might be a helpful illustration. In junior high I had two friend groups: my church friends and my school friends. I had best friends in both spaces and deeply loved both places, so I decided that one year on my birthday I was going to have a huge party at my house and invite *all of them.* Surely, if they all knew and loved me, they would get along and we would become one happy family! It's not that the party ended in disaster or culture clashes, but the segregation was palpable, and I was in inner turmoil the entire evening.

One group of friends was outside in the front yard, hanging out on the lawn, playing basketball, and the other group was gathering in the living room watching a movie. Separate conversations, separate belief systems and ways of living, and yet I was one person holding the tension of both. This is one of the first times I felt that reality of asking, Where do I belong? Little did I know, this kind of feeling was a foreshadowing of what would be a constant for me. I know I am not alone in this, and even today when I think about the people I've gathered close as friends, they don't have much in common. Their beliefs are different, their cultures, races, and experiences are varied, and yet I sometimes desperately want to gather them in a room and see what happens.

What I've recognized about people who inhabit liminal space for a lot of their lives is that they are pretty good at holding space for others—for other beliefs, for other ways of understanding, for questions. I'd say that in the first half of my life, when I was deeply indoctrinated into a kind of Christianity that thrived on fear and dualistic beliefs, I wouldn't have allowed myself to linger in liminal spaces for very long. But as I've gotten older, I'm learning to embrace it, to hold gratitude for the fact that even though I may not always feel I belong or may not fit into the boxes I'm placed in, I belong to those who also don't belong. I belong to myself, in all the nuance and complexity that holds.

It's not as if some of us possess this magical ability of liminality while others don't. We all experience liminality in our lives; that liminality is actually part of the alchemy that makes us human.

Can it be painful to recognize liminal space? Yes. But it's also a gift to know that maybe we don't have to fit into the many colonial boxes set up by society to tell us who we are supposed to be. Maybe the magic is just *who we already are* and *who we are always becoming.*

This is living resistance.

Many of our conversations around liminality have to do with identity, with how we experience ourselves and how we experience the world. Being an Indigenous woman in Christian spaces is often painful for me, as it is for many people who live on the margins of what society deems "normal." As I shared above, liminal space is often painful, even as it is illuminating.

Write down a few ways you've encountered liminal space in your life. If you can't think of anything, explore ways you've noticed liminality around you in the world or in others:

home vs. college
life vs. church
extended fam vs. immediate fam

Palestinian and Brazilian storyteller Jenan Matari gave a powerful TEDx talk on how we embrace identity. She shares about her journey from a painful childhood of not knowing when to belong and how she's learning to love herself well today. "Too often, hyphenated people, minorities, and other people of color are met with claims of 'you're not welcome here' when we embrace our true selves."[1]

So many people are forced by the status quo of our society to live partial lives, or to move throughout their life not fully being present to who they are. Our role as resisters of that status quo is to honor the liminality and complexity of one another's identities.

So liminality is also a political identity.

Conservationist and activist Terry Tempest Williams writes about women's bodies, the earth, and climate collapse: "The story my body wants to tell is a story of love. It is time to lay our bodies down on the Mother and defend her creation—we breathe—we breathe ourselves back into the insistence of Beauty."[2]

Indigenous peoples have been trying to tell a love story about relationship with Mother Earth for a long time, and we've found so much dissonance between our cultures and the cultural norms forced on us; inhabiting these liminal spaces of not being American enough but sometimes not feeling Native enough is very real. We struggle with the ways colonization sneaks up on us, with the ways it has seeped into our veins without our realizing it. So we try our best to hold on to a relationship with Earth, or to heal it, or to ask what happened to it in the first place. We grieve and we celebrate, we dance and we drink water. We remember, and we fiercely heal.

Listening in the liminal spaces helps us recognize dehumanization. If we are all experiencing liminal space somewhere in our lives, our work is to help one another find and embrace that space. We must look for nuance and complexity where it didn't exist before. That means we must break the habit of leaning into stereotypes about one another and instead ask curious, kind questions and practice listening. It also means we find ways not to dehumanize one another.

Like so many aspects of the conversation throughout this book, liminality as it exists in the Ancestral Realm is also about our bodies and the ways we experience liminality through them. As

I mentioned earlier, I am someone who journeys with anxiety, and I am a pretty sensitive person in general, which means I am affected easily by many things, and those effects of stress often manifest in my body.

Learning to recognize the warning signs and lean into healthier patterns has been especially important to me in the last few years. It has helped me understand my own strength in a way I never have before. In 2021, after recognizing that we wouldn't be joining any gyms anytime soon with COVID-19 still on the rise, we bought a Peloton bike. We created a sacred workout/spiritual space that I dearly hoped we'd use. It took me a little while, but I began to realize that in those liminal moments when I am feeling anxious, angry, or stressed, I need a way to get that energy out of my body. I need to jump on a short cycling class, stretch, or, in a particularly liminal season, take a course on boxing.

When you hop on a cycling class, you learn two important terms: *resistance* and *cadence*. Believe me when I say that I knew nothing about cycling when we bought this bike, and for the first few months I felt awful the handful of times I tried a class. As my strength grew in other ways, I was finally ready to try ten-minute, low-impact classes, which are pretty much as easy as it gets, but they were perfect for me.

There, I learned for myself the importance of resistance and cadence, and their relationship. I also learned that being on the bike can be a really sweet liminal space for me. Resistance is how hard it is to pedal: *resisting* the momentum. Cadence is how fast or slow you are going on the bike. The higher the resistance, the harder it is to pedal. If you go at too high a cadence, you'll burn out; it's just too hard. If you go too slow at a high resistance, it's also really hard. At a certain in-between cadence, I am held to a high resistance that also pushes me, allowing me to go at the speed I need to make myself stronger. I trust my body along the way, and by the end, I feel renewed in a way that I haven't felt in many years.

This is how resistance work is too. If we resist too hard and go too fast, we will burn out. If we resist too hard and go too slowly, we'll never get to where we need to go. If we stop resisting and stop moving, the journey is over anyway. But if we find that sweet spot, that liminal space where resistance and cadence meet, where the work and the movement of the work come together, we can do the work as it is intended for us.

So I invite you to consider: What's your resistance level? What's your cadence level? Trust yourself to find out.

I'll leave you with a poem here in the liminal space about our ancestors, a poem about where they exist in the universe around and among us:

> At least for a while,
> we know where to find you,
> traveling across the Milky Way,
> the Spirit Path.
> We look up and see the galaxy,
> full of life and future dreams.
> We remember you
> and we ask who we want to be.
> At least for a little while,
> our grief guides us,
> questions embedded
> with wondering how to go on.
> We look around
> and see that
> you are everywhere
> but not here at all.
> After a while,
> we keep going—
> asking questions,
> taking walks,
> begging for a better world.

All the while
you're there
and we can sense you
constantly,
everywhere and nowhere,
leading us toward
something, anything,
in all the spaces between.

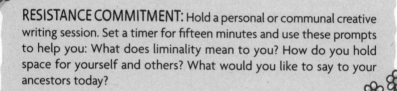

RESISTANCE COMMITMENT: Hold a personal or communal creative writing session. Set a timer for fifteen minutes and use these prompts to help you: What does liminality mean to you? How do you hold space for yourself and others? What would you like to say to your ancestors today?

15

FACING HISTORY AS RESISTANCE

Ordinary people with extraordinary vision can redeem the soul of America by getting in what I call good trouble, necessary trouble.

John Lewis, "Together, You Can Redeem the Soul of Our Nation"

History is personal, communal, and ancestral, which is why I wanted to write about it in this third realm of the book. Throughout history we have heard stories of resistance, of betrayal, of friendship. We have been both encouraged and confused by the actions of our own ancestors. We have wondered who they were in their own day, how they did or did not resist the status quo of hate, apathy, or injustice that surrounded them. Inherently, history is both what our ancestors lived and the current making of history in our lives today, which means, as I've mentioned throughout this book, that

147

we are both the result of our ancestors and on the journey of becoming ancestors ourselves.

History is the in-between space we inhabit right at this very moment. What a heavy, sacred thing, right? With that in mind, here's what I'd like for you to do. Take a few moments to consider three things about history that you've recently discovered or un-learned. Maybe you found out about Indian boarding schools and missionary exploits to colonize Indigenous peoples. Maybe you're learning about rights for and injustices against disabled folks, or you're unlearning about biases toward people of other religions. **Whatever they are, take a moment to write them down here:**

Indian boarding Schools
Doctrine of Discovery

Here's one for me: I didn't grow up knowing about the Doctrine of Discovery. An Indigenous woman who doesn't know the history of colonization on this land? Knowing how history is taught in our schools, this shouldn't come as a surprise. Just as I was taught to admire Columbus and other explorers like him, I was taught that this land was found and kept by the courageous Pilgrims, settlers of the frontier who chose to make a home when and where they could. I was taught that missionary exploits in Christianity have always been destined by God and that those who would refuse salvation deserve the hell they find on the other side.

It has taken a lot of grief and unlearning, not only to under-stand the facts of America as a settler-colonial nation (a popula-tion of settlers displacing and/or replacing the original population of a place) but to go on my own journey of understanding *why* I was denied the truth about my personal history, or about my people's history, and what it might mean for me going forward. How do I resist on a personal, communal, and ancestral level through speaking the truth about history?

First, I am continually working to know my own story, the continually decolonizing truth of who I am: I am Potawatomi, of the People of the Place of Fire, from the Great Lakes region of Turtle Island. I'm also a descendant of European peoples, and understanding that history and how all of my histories combined influence my everyday actions and embodiments.

On the communal level, I fight for families, churches, businesses, colleges, and schools to tell the truth about our history so that our children are better prepared for the future than we ever were. I want to enter academic or spiritual spaces knowing that others understand the founding of this nation, as I continue to learn it. The quote at the beginning of this chapter by Representative John Lewis is a powerful one, written in 2020, when our nation was *still* creating many barriers for Black (and Brown and Indigenous) voters across the country. This is a fight we will continue to have in this country as long as we consider huge portions of our population as less than. Lewis was our representative when we lived in Georgia, and his passion for dancing, for laughing, and for speaking the truth will always inspire me. Getting into *good trouble* is part of the human journey, as is learning to understand why that good trouble is necessary and knowing what truths we must uncover to get there.

Through an ancestral lens, resistance means telling the truth and understanding my ancestors as human beings with trauma and stories, all while understanding that they are held accountable to those actions through my own life. Facing history means facing them in all their humanity, and facing my own in the same way.

Facing history is also about remembering that one day I will be an ancestor, and that truth should keep me tethered to embodying resistance when and where I can. This should be something that guides all of us and reminds us daily that our actions, words, and embodiments have ripple effects into the generations who come after us.

Ever since Trump's presidency in 2017 and through COVID-19 and the time we still find ourselves in, it has felt like we are watching a slow-motion history movie continually playing in front of our eyes, and we are stuck in the theater seats with no way out. Across the United States and even in Canada over the last few years, we saw white supremacy on display again and again, in anti-masking protests and other displays of rugged and toxic individualism. And at the same time, we watched as protests erupted in response to the Supreme Court's decision to end Roe v. Wade or to refuse real action toward gun control and guaranteeing the safety of our children.

As Angela Davis writes, "Progressive struggles—whether they are focused on racism, repression, poverty, or other issues—are doomed to fail if they do not also attempt to develop a consciousness of the insidious promotion of capitalist individualism."[1] Here Davis speaks to the very real struggles of our time and what it means to face history and to choose a different way forward. It is not easy or simple to break toxic cycles, but our refusal to give in to the status quo of hate, racism, or colonialism will help us along the way. We must begin with the refusal, know *why* we refuse, and move toward resistance together.

Black Lakota writer Joy Henderson wrote about anti-masking protests that happened in Canada in 2021, pointing out that the Canadian police were more willing to oppress Black and Indigenous protestors calling for equity and care for the land than the white supremacist protestors filling the streets. She writes, "We are fighting for the state to stop harming us with their state-funded police brutality. We protest for our land to not be destroyed, to repair the harms the state continues to inflict, for clean water."[2]

These are those slow-motion moments in history that many of us remember forever, moments in which toxic individualism and colonialism are held up above human rights and equity. After Roe v. Wade was overturned by the Supreme Court in 2022, our family attended a protest in Philadelphia. At one moment, I found myself marching through the streets with two children on each side of me. Two of them were my own, and the other two, the same age as my kids, were there with their parents; we all chose to bring our kids to the streets to march and name out loud the ways injustice has won and to show that we will keep fighting for a better world. I wish so much for a world where our children aren't coming to protests with us, and yet they are the future-holders, and they will only know the power of their own voices, of the people's voices in changing history, when they use them.

How does resistance happen when we feel like we cannot stop history from repeating itself again and again?

Sometimes we forget that so much of history is storytelling. This is why it is so powerful—when we step back to ask whose stories have been told, we understand how history has been shaped over the years. American history has consistently been the history of white Christian men: the cowboys of the frontier, the settlers' fight for white freedom, the climb those Christian men take to become president, the "hard workers" and loyal voters. History is often *their* story—until we step in and begin telling the other stories, the other truths.

Remembering where we come from, accepting and wrestling with it, and asking what it means for us today are powerful actions. This is why I tell my story and celebrate others who tell their own. When we get the fuller picture of history, we come closer to what community and kinship mean. While there is certainly grief in unlearning mistruths and telling a new or different story, it ends in healing. I truly believe that.

And though I may be biased, I truly believe that books can change history. We know that because schools across the United States are banning books that pose a threat to the myth of a fully equitable, perfect America—they are banning books that tell the truth. In this last chapter discussing the Ancestral Realm, can we commit to some small act of resistance that will change something along the timeline of history? If we remember that history isn't just linear but happens in cycles, then we can disrupt a cycle—a cycle of white supremacy, of ableism, of homophobia, of sexism, of colonialism, of body shaming, of hate. Find your spot on that timeline, within that cycle, and ask what can be done to remind those who come after us, and those who came before, that we care about how history unfolds and that we are willing to make our lives about that care.

Ugandan political activist and poet Dr. Stella Nyanzi knows the truth of using words, stories, and images to resist the status quo of hate. Uganda is a dictatorship where President Museveni has used violence to maintain power since 1986, and people like Stella have resisted for generations. Stella now lives in Germany, where she resists President Museveni from afar. But this came after Stella was arrested and harassed by Museveni's government for calling him out by using what she calls "radical rudeness" and even nudity at times. In an interview with *The Guardian*, she said, "People have said to me: perhaps radical rudeness will not oust Museveni. And I say: perhaps the intention is not to use rude poetry and big breasts in public to oust Museveni; perhaps the idea is to invite others to be able to poke holes in this huge over-glorification of a mighty, untouchable demigod and, if many of us are poking small holes, perhaps the mighty trunk of the tree will fall. I don't know."[3]

Dr. Nyanzi knows both the danger and the strength of the stories that those in power tell to control us. She uses poetry and activism to fight against those stories, to challenge those in power for the sake of a better future. People all over the world who fight for human rights know that challenging the status quo of history is ancestral work, based in kinship and solidarity, and that sometimes it's scary as hell. But we resist anyway.

In fall 2020, we had just moved to Vermont, and, like so many other authors, I was wondering how my words might mean something for the time we were living in. I decided to use Instagram as a medium for storytelling, for conversations grounded in solidarity and kinship. I hosted a series called "Who Is America?" and invited guests whom I deeply admire to tell their story, to describe what or who America is to them and discuss whether they think we can become something different than we have been.

My guests were thoughtful, kind, and fierce, and they fully brought themselves to the conversation. I interviewed academic, activist, and community leader Dr. Twyla Baker about Indigenous joy and the America we have dreamt of for so long. I chatted with my friend Gabes Torres, a therapist and activist, about the power of our stories. Poet Joél Leon spoke with me about the influence we have in our spaces and the power of our words in the time we are living in. Writer and speaker Ruthie Lindsey reminded us to get in touch with our child selves, to love them well and learn to love each other well. The founder of "#blackcoffeewithwhite friends," Marcie Alvis-Walker, talked about the dreams she has for an America where we are truly kin. Afro-Indigenous activist Amber Starks (@melaninmvskoke) and I dreamt about solidarity and the freedom that telling the truth brings. Model, author, and poet Arielle Estoria showed up to the space with grace and laughter, and we honored our own stories together. My friend, Sikh educator and author Simran Jeet Singh, joined me to talk about the violence of the America we know and where we go from here. And therapist Dr. Teri Murphy held space with me as we asked what the pandemic meant to us as Americans and how we can hold each other through it.

The willingness of my conversation partners to show up was deeply empowering, and it reminded me that the stories we tell matter, and they are being told by *so many of us*. Everyone I talked with in the series is living their own way of truth-telling, making space to lean into important conversations in their personal lives, communities, and even online spaces. They are naming the America they've known, and daring to dream of a better one for future generations. *This is resistance.*

RESISTANCE COMMITMENT: Grab a sheet of paper or start a new document on your phone or computer, and begin an ongoing list of questions you have about history. Get in touch with your childlike curiosity. Let yourself begin to wonder at the things you've been taught throughout your life—don't be afraid to unlearn something and to step into new ways of learning. It's never too late to begin something new, to tell the truth when we were missing it. Where will you begin?

Here are a few ideas to get you started: What was the Doctrine of Discovery about? What's the history of abuse toward disabled people in America? How can I learn more about the wisdom of nature? What other religions and cultures do I want to know more about?

PART 4

THE INTEGRAL REALM

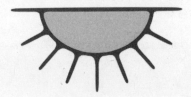

Don't look for anything. Don't look for the meaning of life. Don't look for God. Just *look*—that's all. This is the fundamental quality of a spiritual seeker.

SADHGURU, *Karma: A Yogi's Guide to Crafting Your Destiny*

THE INTEGRAL REALM

is yellow, and it is at the very center of who we are, our *shkode* (fire). In this realm, we integrate all the embodiment, presence, and work of the other realms. The Integral Realm, the season of autumn, is the time to harvest, to gather in all that we've learned, unlearned, and embodied in the other realms.

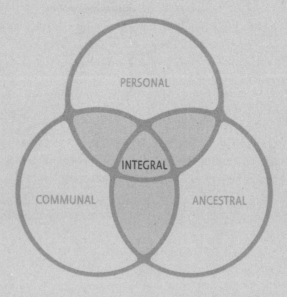

To the tender call of letting go,
I give not an answer
but a breath—
a steady in and out
to admit and accept
that all that is required here
is presence and not sureness.
To the tender call of falling,
I close my eyes
and open my hands,
palms up,
thoughts spanning
the fullness of living and breathing
the depths of everything
that lives and loves.
To the tender call of believing,
I claim not ideology but thisness—
the presence and heartbeat
of body, mind,
and spirit
that always seek.
And to the tender call of embracing,
I simply abandon,
strip bare,
forsake,
so that in all that is left
I am known and fully held
in what I do not know—
that the letting go,
the falling,
the believing,
the embracing,
is in itself all that living gives
from the sunrise to the sunset of every created day,
every created moment,
every created opportunity,
a glimpse of presence and eternity
embodied in this body,
embodied in love.

16

INTEGRATION
AS RESISTANCE

> Rebellion is as much of a cage as obedience is. They both mean living in reaction to someone else's way instead of forging your own. Freedom is not being for or against an ideal, but creating your own existence from scratch.
>
> Glennon Doyle, *Untamed*

Integral means "something that is necessary to make the whole complete." In the fourth realm of resistance, the Integral Realm, everything comes together. The realms of resistance, of *personal*, *communal*, and *ancestral* commitments to resisting the status quo, are meant to flow in and out of one another throughout our lives. *That* is why the overlap, the integration, matters.

The Integral Realm is the realm of harvest, where we gather up the fruit of all that we have worked so hard for and celebrate it. Look at the colored Venn diagrams of the realms on the cover, and notice the golden color at the very center, our soul center. Remember, there will be times when we move back and forth in our other realms, living in more than one realm at once. But this realm is special because it lies at the center of our being and shows us who we are.

In these final chapters, I'll cover topics like interspiritual relationships, prayer, and lifelong resistance. My intention is to guide us out of these pages and into the world with hope for a better way forward.

So let's imagine this overlap. The integration is such a sacred area. It is the space where we bring all of who we are, where there are no binaries that would cause us to feel like we can't fully show up. There is no *this* or *that*, no *us* or *them*. It is a space of total acceptance where we are free to be curious. It is *safe.*

Syilx and Secwepemc writer Elaine Alec shares four conditions for cultivating safe space in her book *Calling My Spirit Back*:

1. Understanding self
2. Working from a love-based place
3. Patience
4. Discipline[1]

Alec is writing about the protocol for a specific type of gathering, but I believe these conditions can also serve as a guide for how we imagine our integral space. In the overlap where all our realms meet, we hold space for understanding ourselves, our life journey. We work from a place of love, we practice patience—with ourselves and others—and we continue to embody discipline in all its forms in our life, in the ways that we move through and navigate resistance. The overlap is a beautiful invitation into the deeply sacred work of integrating all parts of ourselves. As we journey there, let's care for ourselves and one another.

In a way, the Integral Realm is the most mystical of all the spaces because it is where we are fully immersed in the in-between, the liminal space, and we know how powerful that space can be. We are finding the soul of ourselves, the place where we get cracked open, where we stop and ask questions. We are finding that area of our lives where we cannot ignore our pain, where we are faced with the challenge of change and the beautiful possibility of a life marked by resistance.

Perhaps we can think of this integral space through the words of author Matt Haig: "When you stay too long in a place, you forget just how big an expanse the world is. . . . But once you sense that vastness, once something reveals it, hope emerges, whether you want it to or not, and it clings to you as stubbornly as lichen clings to rock."[3]

The Integral Realm is a place of expansiveness, a place where we step out of ourselves, where we hold all of ourselves, where our spiritual center finds its grounding and truly shows us the beauty of the universe.

I've shared in earlier chapters about reconnecting with our child selves, and I want to bring us back to this again as we move into the Integral Realm. Healing the relationship to ourselves is lifelong work.

At a spiritual conference a few years ago, I decided to attend a breathwork session. We were practicing holotropic breathwork, which was created by Stan and Christina Grof in the 1970s. In this type of breathwork (which you should never participate in unless you are with a safe, certified practitioner), participants lie down and practice a series of rapid breaths that put them in an altered state of being for the duration of the process. When I decided to attend the class, I assumed we'd just be sitting there, taking some deep breaths together while listening to classical music. I was wholly unprepared.

After a few minutes of the practice, I was sure nothing was going to happen. Call me a skeptic, but I mostly felt very self-conscious, surrounded by other people also breathing oddly as they lay on their backs. I didn't want to experience anything. Not really. But toward the end of our time, I did.

As I lay there on my back, knees up, I was reminded of the way I had been positioned while giving birth to both of my children. As I lay there, breathing through the memory of every contraction, my body recalled the slow sensation of a coming birth. Then, out of nowhere, a mental image of myself as a young child emerged: I was hiding underneath a table, knees pulled up to my chest, hiding from the environment and world around me that felt like danger and chaos. I was scared and lonely, and no one seemed to notice. This mental image shocked me, and as I continued the breathing exercise, the juxtaposition between that little girl hiding under a table and the woman giving birth became what I am now coming to recognize as an opening to my own Integral Realm, to my heart center, and to an experience of great healing.

I will hold on to that experience forever because it confirmed not only the inner world of anxiety I've held since childhood but the strength I have found in becoming who I am today. It isn't just the physical act of motherhood that has made me stronger but the journeying to figure out who I am, to ask questions, to deconstruct, to engage with myself and others, to set boundaries, to grieve—it is all a gift to my child self, a way of pulling her out from under that table and into my arms, holding her and reminding her that she *is strong* and that resistance will always be a space for her to hold.

Even if you don't do a breathing exercise, pay attention to those moments in your life when your child self and adult self are coming together, or when you're finding grace for seasons in your life that maybe didn't make sense when you were living through them. Through my experience in the breathwork class, I was living in more than one Realm: the Personal, connecting to my child self;

the Ancestral, calling myself out of it and into something else; and the Integral, coming to *integrate* all of it into the ways I love myself and others.

Recently, I spoke to a group of Palestinian children who were studying literature. As we gathered over Zoom, one thing became clear: these children were incredibly talented writers, ready to create a better world. We talked about storytelling, about poetry, and about what inspires us when we are worried about the state of things.

One of the kids typed into the chat that they are asking questions of those who come after them. Can you imagine a twelve-year-old doing this? I can. I can imagine it because I see children every day thinking about how their life will matter when it is over—especially children who come from oppressed communities and who are trying to dream their way out of colonization and hate. Without putting pressure on our children to grow up too soon and lose their sacred childlikeness, our kids are already tapped into that Ancestral Realm in a way we have to climb back to as adults sometimes. Our children are already connecting their present to a future they do not yet understand. As they bring all of who they are to their spaces, they tap into the Integral Realm too.

Can we follow them there? Can we write stories, sing songs, draw pictures, speak words that will lead us on from this moment and this day into whomever and whatever comes next? This is lifelong resistance.

RESISTANCE COMMITMENT: Stop a moment and put your hand on your heart. Take three or four deep breaths. Ask yourself: What is at the center of my life? What do I wish to embody at the center of myself? What does integration feel like?

17

INTERSPIRITUAL RELATIONSHIP AS RESISTANCE

Poet Pádraig Ó Tuama writes about the difference between (and connectedness of) fear and courage in his book *In the Shelter*:

In American Sign Language, the sign for courage implies strength that comes from the body, with both finger-spread hands beginning at the chest and moving out to form the letter "s" for strength. The sign is similar in British Sign Language. What is it about courage that has to come from within? And where within does it come from? What is interesting is that the sign for "fear" in British Sign Language uses the same finger-spread hand and touches the chest. It is as if to imply that the difference between fear and courage is whether what is in you comes to the fore or not. It occurs to me that courage comes from the same place as fear, and where there is fear, there is the possibility of courage.[1]

Interspiritual dialogue involves both fear and courage, especially for those of us who may have grown up in a faith and in an America that constantly teaches us to be afraid of and judge everything that is "other." In the Southern Baptist tradition when I was growing up, our missionary quests were specifically to "reach the lost," which ultimately and purposely created an us-versus-them dynamic with everyone outside our bubble.

Fear is what I carried around inside my mind and spirit for a long time—fear of angering God, fear of losing my friends to hell, fear of doing the wrong things, fear of missing an opportunity to save someone else, fear of letting my parents and pastors down. My religion was a mix of fear and colonialism, not courage and love, and it left me with a hollow sense of myself for many years.

But even when I was young, I held a quiet curiosity about the cultures and faiths of the world around me. Today, I get to gather with people of all backgrounds as we consider what our spiritual lives have to teach one another and what opportunities we can create to make the world a better place. It involves storytelling and honest listening. It involves trading our fear for curiosity and courage, and it is always, always worth it. The word *Interspirituality* was coined by faith leader Wayne Teasdale in his book *The Mystic Heart* and speaks to this embodiment, an expression of unity as people across many different spiritual backgrounds honor one another's journeys.

This interspiritual realm goes beyond human beings. As I've written earlier in the book, Western Christianity paired with capitalism has made Mother Earth and all the creatures around us into products and pests instead of beings whom we are meant to be in relationship with.

So as we think about interspiritual relationships, let's consider what humility looks like in our learning from the creatures around us. When you sit under oak trees, what are you learning from them? When you wake up to the sun, *gises*, what is he teaching you? How do sprouting seeds remind us to keep growing? When the seasons change, how do we honor that shift?

As we begin to integrate everything we've been learning, let's not forget the actual world that holds us. Let's not forget Segmekwe, Earth, our Mother, who has always held us and taught us what it means to live, to rest, to remember, to grieve, to celebrate, and to never give up.

That, of course, is resistance.

Because I am a faith leader, people obviously ask me about my faith and theology a lot. I've lately come to say that I live on the "periphery of Christianity," meaning I exist on the edge of the faith that raised me—not necessarily because I want to but because I am asking so many questions that I have essentially journeyed to the edge of myself. What happens at that edge, I don't know, and I have peace in not knowing, as uncomfortable as it makes others who don't want me there.

In recognizing there is so much to learn, so much to decolonize and *unlearn*, I am holding that space at the edge. I do not currently go to church, and I feel no need to. What exists in me is a growing need to engage in conversations with other people of faith to ask our questions together, to journey to our own edges and see what's there for us as human beings.

But while I'm asking difficult questions of the faith that raised me, I'm recognizing that communities of faith are meant to hold one another up, to demand a better world, to embody radical resistance for one another. Valarie Kaur writes, "Every social justice movement in the United States has been infused with the energy of faith leaders who ignite our moral imagination and connect us with our ability to re-create the world around us."[2]

In early 2021, I began working with an interfaith group of organizers, faith leaders, and academics to form a task force on race and religion for the Aspen Institute. I learned a lot in that space, especially the importance of showing up with the gifts that you have to give. It is easy when we come into these spaces to feel like we aren't doing enough, or to compare ourselves to other leaders or activists, wondering why we can't do it that way.

In this particular group, I noticed that there were people who wanted to slow down the process and lean into the work of unlearning, storytelling, and listening, and there were people who were ready to push us into the urgent work of action through organizing. Both roles are important, and that's exactly why we need one another, to know when to listen and when to push. I also notice that these spaces are often overwhelmingly Christian, which is problematic in many ways. We must make efforts to decentralize Christianity in these conversations and listen to those who haven't been allowed at these tables for a long time.

I belong to bear clan in our Potawatomi culture, as my ancestors did. Bear clan is made up of the keepers of the medicine, and I have learned over the years that my medicine is words. My medicine is stories and books and entering into the lives of others through the power of an idea. Healing can happen through words, and I have to remind myself that this gift is not only enough; it is everything to me. So I bring that to this interfaith and interspiritual work, and I know that when I bring that, I show up to others who are organizing, acting, and dreaming.

We need each other to show up as we are, with the gifts left to us by our ancestors. Even if we don't fully know who our ancestors were, we lean into the ancestral kinship of humanity and ask what it means to love one another well. When we do, we create a holy vision of the world we want to choose day by day. And I believe that, over time, many of those visions will become a reality, bringing us to the sacred center of ourselves as well.

I want to come back to a conversation about social media as we explore this realm of integration together. I've noticed a trend on social media: it is an addiction to trauma stories, and it deeply affects our interspiritual relationships with one another.

On Twitter and Instagram especially, when I post about everyday, celebratory things—playing piano, a new sign in my office that reads *I Choose My Magic*, or some epiphany I've had—it is interacted with less than when I share about being traumatized by Christianity, the daily colonization we deal with as Indigenous people, or a call-out of institutions or organizations that continue to treat us poorly. In the case of the latter posts, lots of folks come with their opinions (some with their support), and by the end of the day, I am completely drained. It took me a long time to figure out why, but eventually I realized that we are often looking for stories of trauma, violence, and colonization to latch on to instead of the celebrations of everyday life that fuel us to do this work. It's one of the most toxic and harmful parts of social media.

I've seen similar things said about Black History Month (and other months that are supposed to highlight or "celebrate" different people groups)—Black leaders, activists, and everyday folks asking to simply be celebrated and listened to, instead of using February as a month to examine trauma with a fine-tooth comb and, *my God*, to tag them in the posts doing so. Not only does this leave Black folks exhausted; it also proves that we are interested only in the stories that drive our anger, trauma, and outrage.

Anger and outrage are absolutely necessary if we want to be people who resist. But do you know what else resistance is driven by?

Celebrating one another's complexity.

Showing up for the small, everyday things.

Tossing out the assumption that we are only our trauma.

Refusing to accept that we are only our colonized selves.

Leaning into hard conversations and paying attention to the others too.

Remembering that we need care for ourselves and each other.

Remembering that social media is a tool not just for trauma but also for care.

Integrating all of who we are—the personal parts, the communal parts, the ancestral parts—requires that we show up fully as ourselves and allow others to show up fully as they are. Because social media thrives on the worst news, the most damaging comments, the trauma, violence, and colonization, it's hard to break away and imagine something different.

But we can. We can embody it every day as we remember the humanity that each of us holds.

It gives me immense hope to know that there are movements of interspiritual healing all around us. *The Altar Within* by Juliet Diaz is a gorgeous devotional focusing on liberating our divine selves. Unlike many other self-help books or how-to guides, Diaz's book is written from a place of recognizing the need for deep healing and integration. She writes, "Modern wellness has worked to distort our truths, profiting from our need for healing while appropriating spiritual and Indigenous cultures, medicine, and wisdom. The wellness industry includes some of the biggest and most successful businesses.... Yes, it only works in favor of white privileged people because it was built that way."[3]

Interspiritual relationships require a living resistance. They require us to lean in and name the violent ways that spiritual practices are stolen and appropriated. They require us to listen, share stories, name truths, and hope for healing. They require us to find our own heartbeat and to sync it once again with the heartbeat of Mother Earth.

RESISTANCE COMMITMENT: What interspiritual relationships do you value most in your life, and what relationships do you hope for in the future? Consider who you follow on social media, what books you read, perhaps what biases you hold toward other cultures and belief systems. How can you take time to engage with the spiritual beings around you, including our nonhuman kin?

18

PRAYER AS RESISTANCE

Throughout my childhood and adult life, I have found myself at times, especially out on walks, wondering how God (or the Great Mystery or the Sacred, as I have begun to change my ideas of who or what they are over time) is doing. In a moment of what I can only describe as protective empathy, I ask, *God, how are you doing—really?* because I cannot know what it's like to be aware of what goes on everywhere, all the time. I cannot imagine what it's like to hold galaxies of grief and joy, passion and exhaustion. I cannot imagine what it might be like to be the essence of the Beginning and to constantly hold time, whatever time is. So I ask, *How are you doing with all this?* And I wait for answers in the wind, at the treetops when I look up. Asking God, Mamogosnan (Creator), or the Divine how they are seems natural to me. But I've noticed so often that we don't ask one another—or when we do, we don't mean it.

Are we allowed to say how we really are, and if we do, can we trust other humans to handle it? I've known some who can, and yet when they ask how I am and really seem to mean it, I am often thrown off guard by their kindness and deep presence.

Ironically, in those moments, I don't *want* to burden them with how I'm really doing. I worry it's too much—this is what we've created for ourselves.

Once, at a dinner party, I ended up in conversation with a woman who travels around the world for work but also deeply loves her family in Atlanta. When she asked me questions about myself, I could see in her eyes a hunger to listen to the experiences of another person. I will never forget that evening, how it caught me by surprise—but also how it made me long to be a better listener. Experiences like that one make me keep asking Creator how they are doing. And every now and then, these experiences lead me to decide to text a friend or, on certain days, to pick up the phone and dial their number. I feel surprised when someone on a Zoom call really wants to know how I'm doing. Prayer can be strange and surprising, as our human connections can be. Yet here we are.

Merriam-Webster defines prayer as "an address (such as a petition) to God or a god in word or thought."[1] In my Southern Baptist upbringing, prayer was not this expansive, though deep down I'd hoped it was. Prayer was the list of sins I'd written in my notebook, exhaustive apologies for not doing a long enough quiet time or not saving my best friend's soul yet. Prayer was crawling on my knees up to a god who stood towering over me with a look of disappointment, the militant-type narcissistic father who knew I could never be good enough but thought he'd try to love me anyway. This is not prayer; it is shackles and torture that limit who the Sacred is and who we are.

I tried so many methods over the years to become a better pray-er. I tried the ACTS method—Adoration, Confession, Thanksgiving, Supplication—but ended up getting bored and then feeling guilty for being bored. I tried different types of prayer journals and devotionals, but their questions felt shallow and forced, as did my answers. More recently, I tried the rosary because *why not?* It didn't really stick either. I was constantly assuming that these "tried and true" ways of praying, and my failure at them, meant I didn't *want* to pray or know God—but maybe it just meant I hadn't found my way yet.

Prayer, in addition to being a request, address, or petition, is also a practice that, like so many other practices, can shift and change over time. Depending on our life season, prayer can be a steady, early morning gathering-in where we spend time with our inner landscape and the landscape of the Sacred; or, it can be random thoughts that we hope find God or Mystery at some point, somehow. It can simply be utterances of "help" or "thank you" when we have nothing else to offer.

I met someone once who is an elder and a retired Episcopal priest, and he described his days to me. His aging parents live with him, and he is the caretaker for his wife, running errands, grabbing medicines, doing the laundry and the dishes. He admitted that prayer is not what it once was for him, and practices of prayer and finding the Divine in the everyday are far different now than when he was young and had fewer worries. His embodiment of prayer as a practice, of prayer as resistance, is seeing the sacredness of these daily errands and chores and of caring for those he loves more than anything.

After all these years of searching, I've realized that prayer is those tiny moments. It's also the poetry that I've been writing since I was young.

The book *A Rhythm of Prayer* is a collection of essays, poems, and prayers gathered by Sarah Bessey from a wide array of women who speak to the concept and practice of prayer. It is a book of resistance because it centers marginalized voices and prayers that challenge the status quo of white supremacy. Because my own relationship to prayer has felt complicated, my offering to the book was a poem about Adventure and how she waits for us with a lantern and wildflowers. She waits to show us the world within ourselves and the world without. I write in the poem:

> But God cannot be given or earned.
> No, God is found.[2]

Maybe prayer is about the search. And it's about the finding, the searching again, the wondering if what we've found is really the answer to anything. I'm okay with that because resistance is about rejecting the status quo that prayer is supposed to look a certain way—white, Christian prayers to a patriarchal Zeus-like character up in the sky, angry and waiting for us to fail. Prayer is and must be so much more than that.

So when I ask God *how are you?* and wait for the wind to blow, I am practicing prayer differently. And when the wind blows and the lapping water of a river answers, Creator asks, *And how are you?* then I remember those tortured journal entries as a child, and I get off my knees and look God in their eyes and breathe in and out, because that's how I am, breathing the silence and the mystery.

To *decolonize* prayer, we have to learn to integrate it into all aspects of our lives until it shows itself as the embodiment of beauty that it already is. Decolonizing prayer also means embracing a *queer spirituality* that, as Mihee Kim-Kort writes, "challenges the compartments that we, not God, have created."[3] In other words, we reject colonial boundaries and rules forced on us, and we love one another, ourselves, Mother Earth, and the Sacred freely, wholly, fully. We pray with that freedom.

Embodying prayer as a practice, as a way home, leads us into a fluidity in our ways of being, encouraging us to let go of the boundaries we have set up around who is allowed to pray and how. We find intimacy with the Divine. Like prayer, spirituality is "the real deal," as Rabbi Danya Ruttenberg writes. It is "the impulse undergirding every religious tradition out there. . . . It isn't about the easy and sweet . . . but rather encompasses the anger and the frustration and the ambivalence."[4]

So it goes with prayer, an embodiment of everything that we are, rejecting the boxes that are created from the toxic status quo of colonization, patriarchy, and hate. Instead, we breathe resistance in and out and realize it was prayer the whole time.

I know a small part of a very long Potawatomi prayer that has lived in my body for a few years now. I write in my book *Native* about the moment when I found out that we have not only our own language but our own prayers:

> I stood there with tears in my eyes, because the things I did not yet understand were the things I seemed to so desperately need: to speak the language spoken by my ancestors, years ago, before we were forced out of our home, before we were assimilated into a white culture that wanted only English spoken. The first thing I memorized was a Potawatomi prayer, one that I use often instead of praying in English. It gives me a different space with Creator, *Mamogosnan*, Great Mystery, *Kche Mnedo* than I've had before, a space I cannot reach in any white American church.[5]

Even today, praying in Potawatomi, not just alone but with my children, is resistance in every way. As our people have been colonized throughout the centuries, languages have been taken, which means our ways of praying have also been taken. But we hold onto them, knowing that they are a sacred connection not only to one another but to God, Mamogosnan, Kche Mnedo. I have friends all over the world who are reclaiming the Indigenous prayers and spiritual practices of their ancestors, and it brings me so much hope to see this happening. We are refusing the status quo of whiteness that tells us we must pray in a certain way to a certain kind of God, and in the spirit of integration, we are welcoming all of who we are into that mystery, right at the center of our being. *This is resistance.*

Those Potawatomi prayers, spoken in my ancestors' language, all happen in my home, and I've realized over the years that I am constantly breathing prayer into the spaces we inhabit. We are a family of six (two adults, two kids, two dogs), so it's always a lively place. We've moved a lot in our fourteen years of marriage (eight different homes in five different cities), and every time I've stepped into a new rental house, I've begun praying as I imagine where the couch might go, who will sleep in what room, what corners will be filled with sacredness and kindness. I open my home-decorating books and gather ideas but quickly realize that my styles never quite match theirs. Yet even as I've struggled over the years with not having any particular style that defines my taste, I've learned to embrace my eclectic ways of being and living and let those, too, be prayer.

I petition God, Mystery, Mamogosnan, to be present and full in our spaces as I vacuum the dog hair off the couch or tidy up my home office. I petition the Universe to hold us as we grieve in the kitchen or dance in the living room, as we sleep and dream. Building *home* is the perfect integration of all realms—the Personal, the Communal, and the Ancestral, all coming together. It is where we find self-love, where we practice community with others, especially around the dinner table. It is where we ask our ancestors difficult questions and practice being ancestors ourselves. It is where we hold up the mirror and look deep into our own eyes and stories and ask what resistance means. *We live resistance right there. We pray it right there.*

RESISTANCE COMMITMENT: Reimagine prayer for yourself. Maybe it happens the next time you tidy up the kitchen or wash dishes. Maybe it happens at night when you can't sleep. Maybe it's happening when you're studying for a test or laughing at a joke or staring out a window. Let yourself imagine and embody what prayer is, might be, has always been.

19

DREAMING
AS RESISTANCE

As we near the end of our journey together, I am so glad we are here to explore how dreaming is a tool for resistance. When we were trying to figure out the subtitle for this book, I came to realize I was thinking with a colonial mindset. I first thought that within these pages I'd created a "framework." While that may be true, I realized after a few conversations with my partner, Travis, and with help from the team at my publishing house that the pages of this book, the realms and embodiments here, the commitments to living resistance, are all a *vision*. When I first saw that word introduced into the subtitle, I worried that it was too soft or even weak, not strong—like a framework.

I had to take a step back and pay attention to what I was saying to myself. *An Indigenous Vision for Seeking Wholeness Every Day* may not get me into the door of a conference room where I can present this book to a group of white, cis-gendered executives like a "framework" might. But creating a *vision* is holy work, deep and strong work that goes beyond a framework or an idea, beyond a conference room. It is cyclical and fluid, not structured and limiting. A vision lives and breathes; it is a way forward, a dream that is sure to come. And that's what we have here, because every day we *will seek this vision, this dream*. Remember those words from the beginning of the book?

I am a human being. I am always arriving.

We've arrived here, toward the end of this book's journey, which is, of course, also the beginning. It's all connected, all ebbing and flowing, all cyclical and sacred. So stop for a moment and think about three dreams you have: for us, for Mother Earth, for yourself. **Write or draw them below:**

- I dream that we can save the planet
- I can come to terms w/ what I've been through
- everyone can have access to what they need

Dreams are so powerful—both our literal dreams, the dreams we have at night while we are sleeping, and the daydreaming that keeps us moving forward in our waking hours. Dreams are intergenerational and stretch across cultures, faiths, and beliefs. Dreams carry us.

I sometimes use the Calm app to fall asleep peacefully, and one of my favorite soundscapes is coffee shop sounds. One of the most comforting things I can imagine is sitting in my favorite shop, writing, as people hustle and bustle around me. The reality is, this book was mostly written from the quiet of my home—my home in Vermont and my home in Philadelphia. Twice I escaped to a hotel room ten minutes from my home to look outside at a river and our city, to get these thoughts down before I felt like they were going to disappear forever.

These pages have been written from my bed, the living room couch, the backyard under the pergola. A few times I've made it to the coffee shop, but mostly, I've been writing in quiet isolation. In these moments, these days, dreaming is listening to the coffee shop soundscape and imagining some future day when I work on a writing project as I build community with a local shop and get to know others around me, even if I never actually talk to them. Sometimes our dreams are built in the quiet like that.

Vermont was the place that let me ask who I want to be. I began a professional writing career quickly—after receiving my first book deal, I jumped right in, releasing my second book a few years later. While growing a social media following, I traveled around the country to speak on topics of identity, spirituality, and decolonization.

The problem is, at some point, instead of you becoming the work, the work becomes you: labels and boxes and the opinions and ideas of others tell us who we are, and we accept it for a while, until we burn out and are forced to ask if we have become someone else in the process.

It's not that I lost myself to the work of being an author—indeed, I found my voice in ways I never thought possible—but the habits created in my early years (a lot of them due to trauma) have followed me into my career until I learned to face them and heal from them. I was afraid to say no to things. I was worried about coming on too strong or appearing too angry. I let social media dictate my voice at times, instead of recognizing it as the tool it is meant to be.

So in the quiet of rural Vermont, my days of composting and gardening, of lighting the wood stove and walking the dogs and taking long drives, gave me pause to examine how I want to be in this world. It was an integral space for our family and for my soul to ask what's next.

In dreaming, I needed to commit to equipping myself with the right tools. I needed to name that I am fierce yet gentle, childlike yet wise. I am a woman learning to love her body well and struggling along the way. I am an Anishinaabe *kwe* asking my ancestors to guide me. I am moved by ceremony. I need healthy relationships with boundaries. I want to be happy.

I bought a red journal that I started writing my needs in, the things I knew I had to have moving forward—things like saying no more often, asking what I really enjoy, speaking up for myself when something is unreasonable, and remembering that I am not too much.

Sometimes we need a full change of scenery (or, worst case, a global pandemic) to trap us with ourselves in a room and force us to ask who we are supposed to be. Sometimes, though, those little epiphanies meet us wherever we are and ask us to look deeper. Dreaming is an act of resistance in every way because it keeps us from giving up on ourselves and the community of people who hold and support us. Dreaming keeps us moving toward another way, toward future generations, somehow toward our ancestors, and toward healing, the earth, and ourselves.

My book *Native* is all about dreaming of a better world on the other side of this collapsing one. The Potawatomi flood story, like many such stories, tells the tale of Creator flooding the earth and of the animals (and Original Man) working to create one again. Our Potawatomi story features the muskrat and turtle, who make it possible to dream of a future world that can be created from dirt and shell. That's why we need those stories, especially when it's hard to dream for ourselves. We need stories from all over the world to tell us that it's worth it to dream, even when it feels impossible to do so.

Author Arundhati Roy writes about this time we are in—not only a time of a worldwide pandemic but also a time in which we continue to fight for a better and more equitable world. She says, "We can choose to walk through it, dragging the carcasses of our prejudice and hatred, our avarice, our data banks and dead ideas, our dead rivers and smoky skies behind us. Or we can walk through lightly, with little luggage, ready to imagine another world. And ready to fight for it."[1]

Dreaming can be a very scary endeavor. Choosing that vision and refusing to let go can be overwhelming. That is why we carry our dreams here, into this Integral Realm, into the core of ourselves. We hold our dreams so carefully—the personal dreams, the communal dreams, the ancestral dreams. Institutions may crumble along the way. White supremacy may shift and fall little by little or, sometimes, may grow and metastasize. Still, we hold those dreams and visions to our chest, and we do not let go.

Remember Soul Fire Farm, the Afro-Indigenous farm that we looked at as an example of intergenerational healing work? They started that movement and that work because of a dream, a vision.

The twelve-year-old Palestinian students I chatted with about poetry and colonization are dreaming up a new world through words and ideas, and their passion is endless.

Indian farmers dream of a connection to the land and their own bodies that isn't taken by the government or corporations.

We dream through ritual and ceremony, through practices that ground us here but also usher us forward into whatever comes next. Can we dream and envision without getting trapped in one way of doing things? As we live into resistance, can we let those dreams transform or change as they need to? Can we edit those visions while holding to the spirit that brought them forward in us? This, too, is resistance.

I lead a workshop on holding space in difficult times, and in this workshop we focus on three areas: holding space for ourselves, holding space with Mother Earth, and holding space with other humans.

As we close out this chapter, think about these three ideas. How have you held space for yourself lately? When I began trauma therapy, I noticed how uncomfortable I am with the silence that falls sometimes between my therapist and me. Sitting in that room, sitting with the air, with our breathing, with our eye contact (or lack thereof) forces a reality that our souls are meant to be listened to and cared for, even if we aren't speaking. Taking a moment of silence for ourselves produces space and room to be present with others as our full selves.

As we've been learning throughout this book, holding space with Mother Earth is an essential part of our resistance journey. As humans, we go about our lives not always conscious of the land we exist on, the water we drink, the food we eat. Take a moment to think about what you had for breakfast this morning or the coffee you drank to wake up. Think about the origins of that food, the very seeds those coffee beans came from, or the fruit tree that grew to give us its bounty. We must learn to hold space with Mother Earth as we resist and as we dream.

Holding space with other people is difficult—which is why this whole journey is so essential. When we lean into the power of the *story*, we take the time to hold space, to be present, to put down the phones and other distractions, and to simply listen. We are created for kinship, for holding space with one another, but sometimes we have to work at getting back to that place.

Our stories, our connection to this Earth, and the ways we learn to embody the work of resistance are all leading us toward wholeness, toward integration, every single day. As Cole Arthur Riley writes in *This Here Flesh*, "Our dignity may involve our doing, but it is foremost in our very being—our tears and emotions, our bodies lying in the grass, our scabs healing."[2]

We hold our dignity. We hold Mother Earth's dignity. We hold each other's dignity. This is *always resistance*.

RESISTANCE COMMITMENT: On a piece of paper, draw circles that represent different seasons of your life, and spend some time remembering and writing down the different dreams you've held through the years. Maybe those dreams didn't happen. Maybe they were shattered. That's okay. Hold space for yourself to grieve those dreams. Write down the dreams you hold now. Honor them. Don't let go.

20

LIFELONG RESISTANCE

It is January 14, 2022.

I am in my bedroom, door shut, afternoon sunlight streaming through the windows, dogs barking in the background. The kids are at home doing school virtually. Winter jazz music is playing from a YouTube channel on my laptop, and I should be working on a book about everyday resistance.

But I can't.

I can't write because the cobwebs that have covered every corner of my mind are difficult to clear out. We've been in a global pandemic for over two years as of this writing, and it is taking its toll on us, still. The hardest part is that I can do nothing about it. I can't do anything about the dogs barking, or the kids in virtual school, or the cobwebs. I am tired, and though I don't feel I've run out of words, I do struggle with how to organize them once they come out of my head and heart and onto the page.

It's like I am trapped in a stream of consciousness that I deeply need to sort through, and nothing more. I need space to sift through the words and ideas, time to ask what the images mean or don't mean. And yet I sit here on the verge of tears, feeling like I have no idea what resistance even is right now. To *resist* the status quo, right now, in the midst of *this*? How? Where? Why?

So I step back a moment and reconsider everything I've learned about difficult seasons, about grief.

We don't always know when grief will come.

We cannot always control the seasons.

We must always, always trust our bodies to tell us the truth.

We remember that grieving takes time.

We take a few deep breaths, no matter what.

We try again when we're ready.

So pause. Breathe.

Let's begin again.

Resistance is surprisingly flexible: sometimes when I feel like I can't, I need to rest, and sometimes when I feel like I can't, I need to write and lean in. And both can be true at the same time. Resistance, much like happiness or joy, isn't about having certain prerequisites. Living resistance doesn't always mean that I have both feet on the ground, but it does mean that I am grounded nonetheless. Resistance is about being honest about who I am and who I am not, about how I am doing and what I am capable of at any moment. Author and CNN analyst Kirsten Powers writes in her book *Saving Grace*, "There were the rare birds I knew who seemed to embody grace. . . . I noticed they had a few things in common: They were spiritually grounded and humble. They had done the work of self-examination, getting real with themselves about their limitations, and doing the work to address them."[1]

Many of us have been reeling and in traumatized fight, flight, or freeze mode for the past few years as the world has looked different than it did before. We will spend our entire lives asking what resistance means for us. But in this moment, wherever we are, we must ask: What does resistance mean for me *right now*?

It means taking my dog for a walk.

It means checking in with my kids.

It means eating a healthy meal or snack.

It means supporting my friend Shel's Patreon as she creates incredible music.

It means crying when I need to cry.

It means encouraging another writer to keep going.

It means recognizing my limitations today, tomorrow, and in the coming days.

It means saying *I am a human being. I am always arriving.*

Turns out, resistance is simply choosing to arrive.

We have arrived, but we are still arriving.

I hope you have learned some things about yourself here. I hope it is just your beginning in many ways—I feel as if it is a kind of beginning for me too.

I noticed something odd about myself a few years back, and Travis teases me about it when he gets the chance. For some reason, I often leave *one last piece of food* on my plate after I have eaten. Whatever the meal, the fruit, the drink—for some reason I don't finish the whole thing. Have I been saving it for another time? Was it some sort of trauma response from when I was young? Maybe I was keeping it in case we ran out of food? I have no idea, but it's made me curious.

I used to do the same thing with exercise. I'd get off the stationary bike about five minutes before my ride was over, or I'd stop trying as I got to the end. I do it less now, but only because I have noticed the pattern and want to break it. Still, it is kind of odd, isn't it?

The same can be said about this journey of resistance, that we often stop before we've reached a really pivotal moment, or that we long for a solid change in the *ways* we resist. Resistance can be, and often will be, difficult. Remember, our human journey is lifelong, and it's meant to ebb and flow, to change as our life seasons change. Even though that's true, please don't give up before the end. Please keep going and finish the song, finish the dance, take the last glorious bite. We will always be living this life until we're not—and still our ripple effects live on.

We are always arriving. But make sure you actually arrive, even if it's just to the next step of the journey.

As I mentioned at the beginning of the book, I am a writer who speaks and reflects on identity. And while it is important on many levels for us to figure out who we are, we also somehow have to find the courage and space to move _beyond_ identity. What is at the essence of who we are? This is really what the integration is all about, isn't it?

I love the words of Rabbi Alan Lew in _This Is Real and You Are Completely Unprepared_: "We spend a great deal of time and energy propping up our identity, an identity we realize at bottom is really a construct. So it is that we are always living at some distance from ourselves. We live in a fearful state of siege, trying to prop up an identity that keeps crumbling, that we secretly intuit to be empty. . . . But something persists—something fundamentally nameless and empty, something that remains when all else has fallen away."[2]

I want to end this book as we started it, keeping in mind that the circles we travel on, the realms we inhabit—whether personal, communal, ancestral, or the center space where they all overlap—are forever teaching us the same lessons. They offer us lessons about what it means to begin again, what it means to come home to ourselves, what it means to become people who love better and live fully.

Along the way, identities matter as we work out who we are. But at the same time, when all those identities fall away and we are left with only the soul of ourselves, our true essence, we have to ask: _What's there? Who's there?_ What do you have to teach yourself? How does your soul, when it is allowed to simply be a soul, guide you? And do you hold space for yourself to know that this is a lifelong journey of transformation and listening?

I learn so much from the activists, resisters, artists, and prophets who lead us every single day in this embodiment, reminding us that this truly is lifelong work that we honor in our bodies, minds, and spirits. Tarana Burke, founder of the "'me too.' Movement" (Burke's movement was co-opted by the #MeToo Movement, but they are not the same thing) writes about her own sense of calling in her book *Unbound*: "My lessons are never low-key and my assignment is always plain and clear once it is revealed. I am hardwired to respond to injustice. It doesn't always sit well with me, but I've learned the hard way not to ignore it. It's the same wiring that led to the creation of the 'me too.' Movement."[3]

Burke knows how it feels when the assignment is clear, and though we may go through seasons when we are unsure and that assignment brings struggle, something truly magical happens when it all clicks, when we become informed of our own sacred calling, when we know exactly what it is we are to do in this world, for ourselves and for one another. There, in the integration of our personal, communal, and ancestral embodiments, we find out exactly who we are, and we continue the lifelong journey of honoring that every single day.

This is resistance.

An important part of the lifelong work of resistance is to understand both what we are responsible for and what we are not responsible for. It is not our responsibility to take on every single thing all the time. It takes courage to stop and ask what work is ours to do, what healing is for us to embody along the way. It means having the courage to say no to what isn't ours so that we can say yes to everything that is, and say yes without fear.[4] It also means we learn how to be subversive in the face of toxic and oppressive institutions.

Undermining the authority or power of an institution—this is what so much of our resistance work is truly about. We live in nations that run on institutions and systems, spaces that are full of abusive power and oppressive authority.

The question for many of us is whether to stay or to go, and it is always a complicated decision. Do we stay, hoping to change often toxic and abusive systems or institutions from within, sometimes giving decades of our lives to the cause? Or do we go, forging a new path, looking for a better way, hoping to God it exists out there and is waiting for us?

I cannot answer these questions for anyone else, but they're worth asking so that we can understand what's at stake, whatever we decide. I hope that those who choose to stay have the support systems they need, or at least know they are not alone. I hope that they learn how to be subversive, holding steady to the work of resistance, whatever it looks like for them. For those who go, I hope they find places that hold and cherish them for who they are, that give them space to dream about and build a better world.

In his book *The Future Earth: A Radical Vision for What's Possible in the Age of Warming*, Eric Holthaus encourages us to ask ourselves a few questions in the face of climate disasters:

> What is my vision of a better world?
> What steps need to happen for it to become a reality?
> Starting today, where do I fit in that vision?[5]

Resistance is a lifelong endeavor, and so is the act of dreaming. We have been given a certain kind of world, we have helped create a certain kind of world, and we get to dream of what kind of world we want to exist in our future years and after we are gone. *This* is where the realms overlap, where the space between becomes the center of everything. Who we are becoming today, the ways we choose healing for ourselves and our communities, and the lines of people who came before and will come after—it all matters.

So plant the garden. Tell the story. Go to therapy and pay for someone else to go too. Text a friend and let them know you have not forgotten them. Ask someone not to forget you. Look into your dog's eyes and exchange kinship. Tell Mother Earth you love her and receive that love back. Challenge the status quo. Learn about what's happening in the world. Water your house plants. Take a walk or look out a window. Listen to music. Create. Tell the truth. Forgive yourself. Decolonize. Live your life in the overlapping spaces where it all comes together, and *dream*. Resistance is for you. Resistance is for us. We were made for this. I believe in Us.

RESISTANCE COMMITMENT: Read these words and sign your name at the bottom as a commitment to embodying lifelong resistance. Add a few to the list if you'd like.

> How do we resist?
> We resist by breathing,
> by gardening,
> by telling the truth,
> by reading banned books,
> by singing love songs,
> by grieving,
> by trying again,
> by not giving up on ourselves,
> by challenging what we think we know,
> by knowing that love is always there,
> by trusting future generations,
> by drawing pictures,
> by fighting ableism,
> by petting dogs,
> by telling your body they matter,
> by sending flowers to a tired friend,
> by reaching out when you might need flowers,
> by dreaming of an anti-racist world,
> by meditating when things get hard,
> by being patient with yourself,

by setting healthy boundaries,
by believing in solidarity,
by refusing to "other" your kin,
by writing in that journal,
by saying hello to Mother Earth every day,
by listening to music,
by writing music,
by deconstructing what you once knew,
by asking what it all means,
by admitting we know nothing,
by honoring humility,
by honoring the children,
by becoming like children,
by dancing in a snowstorm,
by holding someone's hand,
by holding your own hand,
by breathing deep (again),
by saying yes to all the magic that is,
by saying no to the status quo of harm,
by honoring whatever realm you are in,
by honoring all the spaces in between,
by honoring this moment, this time, this embodiment.
This is *living resistance*.

_____ (your name)

ACKNOWLEDGMENTS

Writing a book during COVID-19 was no simple thing, and I am so grateful to have made it here. I'm so grateful to Segmekwe, Mother Earth, for holding and tending to my spirit, to Creator for giving me gentle nudges to keep going.

I'm so grateful to my family: Travis, Eliot, and Isaiah, and our dogs, Jupiter and Blaze, who help me keep my dreams alive and who have never doubted me for a second. You keep me laughing, playing, breathing deep, and remembering why it all matters.

I will be forever grateful to every author whose books I read to prepare me for this moment, for the wisdom you hold and share with the world. I hold so much love and respect for your work.

To my agents Jim and Rachelle, who fight for my voice and my work to succeed in this world. To Alanah for designing the incredible cover, and to the entire Brazos team: you've always believed in me and let me speak the truth, and I'm so grateful for that. And thank you to Amy Paulson for always capturing my very spirit in your photos.

To friends who processed with me along the way: Kelley, Asha, Shel and Mel, Simran, Brenda, Patty, Meg and Brooke, Danya,

Amena, Meredith, Rachel, Daniel, and so many others—thank you for holding this space with me.

To the lands that held me as I wrote this book: Vermont, the land of the Abenaki and Wabanaki peoples and the sacred waters that held us, and Philadelphia, Lenape land, a bustling and beautiful city and its waters that welcomed us right away, you provided a way for me and I will never forget that.

And to every reader: your journey matters, and I am so honored to be a part of it. May you find ways to live resistance however you can in the pages of this book and out there in the beautiful, terrible world.

NOTES

Introduction

1. To learn more about this, look to Mirabai Starr's book *God of Love: A Guide to the Heart of Judaism, Christianity, and Islam* (Rhinebeck, NY: Monkfish, 2012).

2. "Our Values," We Are Sikhs, 2017, http://www.wearesikhs.org/values.

3. "Definition of Humanism," American Humanist Association, 2022, https://americanhumanist.org/what-is-humanism/definition-of-humanism/.

4. If you'd like to learn more about the Seven Grandfather Teachings, this website is a helpful guide: https://www.7generations.org/seven-grandfather-teachings/.

Chapter 1 What Is Resistance?

1. Sadhguru, *Karma: A Yogi's Guide to Crafting Your Destiny* (New York: Harmony Books, 2021), 34.

2. *Oxford English Dictionary*, s.v. "story," accessed June 28, 2022, https://www.lexico.com/en/definition/story.

3. Julie Rodgers, *Outlove: A Queer Christian Survival Story* (Minneapolis: Broadleaf Books, 2021), 5.

4. Austen Hartke, *Transforming: The Bible and the Lives of Transgender Christians* (Louisville: Westminster John Knox, 2018), 109.

5. "Fatal Violence against the Transgender and Gender Non-Conforming Community in 2021," Human Rights Campaign, 2021, https://www.hrc.org/resources/fatal-violence-against-the-transgender-and-gender-non-conforming-community-in-2021.

6. Mia Birdsong, *How We Show Up: Reclaiming Family, Friendship, and Community* (New York: Hachette, 2020), 14.

Chapter 2 Art as Resistance

1. Sydney Stevenson, "Art as Resistance: Turning Beauty into Power," *Grass-roots Journal*, February 13, 2020, https://www.thegrassrootsjournal.org/post/2019/11/17/art-as-resistance-turning-beauty-into-power.

2. DisArt Mission Statement, accessed January 20, 2022, https://www.disartnow.org/about/mission/.

3. Niela Orr, "What Does the Raised Fist Mean in 2017?," Buzzfeed News, February 1, 2017, https://www.buzzfeednews.com/article/nielaorr/what-does-the-raised-fist-mean-in-2017.

4. Asha Frost, *You Are the Medicine: 13 Moons of Indigenous Wisdom, Ancestral Connection, and Animal Spirit Guidance* (Carlsbad, CA: Hay House, 2022), 7.

5. Joel Brown, "'Jingle Bells' History Takes Surprising Turn," BU Today, December 8, 2016, https://www.bu.edu/articles/2016/jingle-bells-history/.

Chapter 3 Presence as Resistance

1. Leanne Betasamosake Simpson, *As We Have Always Done: Indigenous Freedom through Radical Resistance* (Minneapolis: University of Minnesota Press, 2017), 103.

2. Robin Wall Kimmerer, *Braiding Sweetgrass: Indigenous Wisdom, Scientific Knowledge, and the Teachings of Plants* (Minneapolis: Milkweed, 2015), 222.

3. Guy Winch, "10 Real Risks of Multitasking, to Mind and Body," *Psychology Today*, June 22, 2016, https://www.psychologytoday.com/us/blog/the-squeaky-wheel/201606/10-real-risks-multitasking-mind-and-body.

4. Tricia Hersey, "Rest Is Anything That Connects Your Mind and Your Body," The Nap Ministry, February 21, 2022, https://thenapministry.wordpress.com/2022/02/21/rest-is-anything-that-connects-your-mind-and-body/.

5. Suleika Jaouad, *Between Two Kingdoms: A Memoir of a Life Interrupted* (New York: Random House, 2021), 234.

Chapter 4 Embodiment as Resistance

1. Hillary McBride, *The Wisdom of Your Body: Finding Healing, Wholeness, and Connection through Embodied Living* (Grand Rapids: Brazos, 2021), 7.

2. Kat Armas, *Abuelita Faith: What Women on the Margins Teach Us about Wisdom, Persistence, and Strength* (Grand Rapids: Brazos, 2021), 150.

3. Christine Platt, "Women Who Inspire: Christine Platt—the Afrominimalist," March 9, 2021, *Shira Gill* (blog), https://shiragill.com/christine-platt-the-afrominimalist/.

Chapter 5 Radical Self-Love as Resistance

1. Najwa Zebian, *Welcome Home: A Guide to Building a Home for Your Soul* (New York: Harmony Books, 2021), 58.

2. Nedra Glover Tawwab, *Set Boundaries, Find Peace: A Guide to Reclaiming Yourself* (New York: TarcherPerigee, 2021), 64.

3. Tawwab, *Set Boundaries*, 25.

4. Rabbi Alan Lew, *This Is Real and You Are Completely Unprepared: The Days of Awe as a Journey of Transformation* (New York: Little, Brown, 2003), 119.

5. adrienne maree brown, *Pleasure Activism: The Politics of Feeling Good* (Chico, CA: AK Press, 2019), 59.

Chapter 6 Childcare as Resistance

1. Latinx Parenting (@latinxparenting), "It takes a village? It takes affordable housing. It takes access to mental health," Instagram, November 29, 2021, https://www.instagram.com/p/CW2heUnrfQR/.

2. Elissa Welle, "Detroit Police Break Up Native Sugarbush Ceremony, Saying 'Sovereign Stuff Is Not Valid,'" *Detroit Free Press*, February 22, 2022, https://www.freep.com/story/news/local/michigan/detroit/2022/02/19/detroit-police-break-up-native-ceremony/6861547001/.

3. Rebecca Nagle, "Solomon's Sword," August 23, 2021, in *This Land*, produced by Crooked Media, podcast, MP3 audio, 47:17, https://crooked.com/podcast/1-solomons-sword/.

4. Alexandra Payan, "ICWA's Constitutionality Challenged and Review by Supreme Court Underway," March 11, 2022, National Council of Urban Indian Health, https://ncuih.org/2022/03/11/icwas-constitutionality-challenged-and-review-by-the-supreme-court-underway/.

5. bell hooks, *All about Love: New Visions* (New York: HarperCollins, 2001), 30.

6. "Walking the Walk Youth Initiative," Interfaith Philadelphia, last accessed February 12, 2022, https://www.interfaithphiladelphia.org/youth-initiatives.

Chapter 7 Ethical Practices as Resistance

1. Kaitlin B. Curtice, *Native: Identity, Belonging, and Rediscovering God* (Grand Rapids: Brazos, 2020), 156.

2. Mirabai Starr, *Wild Mercy: Living the Fierce and Tender Wisdom of the Women Mystics* (Boulder, CO: Sounds True, 2019), 70.

3. Susanna Barkataki, *Embrace Yoga's Roots: Courageous Ways to Deepen Your Yoga Practice* (Orlando: Ignite Yoga & Wellness Institute, 2020), 9.

4. Barkataki, *Embrace Yoga's Roots*, 45.

5. Tejal Yoga, last accessed November 15, 2021, https://tejalyoga.com/herstory.

6. "V-Day Is a Global Activist Movement," V-Day, last accessed July 1, 2022, https://www.vday.org.

7. Terry Tempest Williams, "Rejoice & Rise 2022," One Billion Rising, streamed live on February 14, 2022, YouTube video, at 41:37–47:53, https://www.youtube.com/watch?v=CXsPmKtVBGs.

8. Kimmy Yam, "NYPD Reports 361 Percent Increase in Anti-Asian Hate Crimes since Last Year," NBC, December 10, 2021, https://www.nbcnews.com /news/asian-america/nypd-reports-361-percent-increase-anti-asian-hate -crimes-last-year-rcna8427.

9. Frances Kai-Hwa Wang, "How Violence against Asian Americans Has Grown and How to Stop It, according to Activists," PBS News Hour, April 11, 2022, https://www.pbs.org/newshour/nation/a-year-after-atlanta-and-indianap olis-shootings-targeting-asian-americans-activists-say-we-cant-lose-momentum.

10. Curtice, *Native*, 21.

Chapter 8 Solidarity Work as Resistance

1. *Merriam-Webster Online Dictionary*, s.v. "solidarity," accessed February 12, 2022, https://www.merriam-webster.com/dictionary/solidarity.

2. Debbie Woodin, "Joplin Man Pleads Guilty in Mosque Fire, Clinic Arsons," *Joplin Globe*, April 18, 2016, https://www.joplinglobe.com/news/local _news/updated-joplin-man-pleads-guilty-in-mosque-fire-clinic-arsons/article _ef7b3174-85e1-59c4-86c0-dac07a5cffb4.html.

3. "Religious Pluralism 101," Aspen Institute, July 17, 2019, https://www .aspeninstitute.org/blog-posts/religious-pluralism-101/.

4. Kristin Kobes Du Mez, *Jesus and John Wayne: How Evangelicals Corrupted a Faith and Fractured a Nation* (New York: Liveright, 2020), 12.

5. Frank Edwards, Hedwig Lee, and Michael Esposito, "Risk of Being Killed by Police Use of Force in the United States by Age, Race-Ethnicity, and Sex," *Proceedings of the National Academy of Sciences* 116, no. 34 (2019): 16793–98.

6. Travis B. Curtice and Brandon Behlendorf, "Street-Level Repression: Protest, Policing, and Dissent in Uganda," *Journal of Conflict Resolution* 65, no. 1 (2021): 166–94.

7. Krenak Naknanuk, "Repression by the Police in Brazil, as Bill PL 490 Threatens Indigenous Rights," Cultural Survival, June 24, 2021, https://www .culturalsurvival.org/news/repression-police-brazil-bill-pl-490-threatens -indigenous-rights.

8. Tish Harrison Warren, "Why Churches Should Drop Their Online Services," January 30, 2022, https://www.nytimes.com/2022/01/30/opinion /church-online-services-covid.html.

9. Kaitlin Curtice (@kaitlincurtice), "I really hoped that this pandemic would have us . . . ," Twitter, January 31, 2022, 10:38 a.m., https://twitter.com/Kait linCurtice/status/1488174741718552580.

10. June Eric-Udorie, "When You Are Waiting to Be Healed," in *Disability Visibility: First-Person Stories from the Twenty-First Century*, ed. Alice Wong (New York: Vintage Books, 2020), 53–58.

11. Alicia T. Crosby (@aliciatcrosby), "As I said before, the Church/US American Christianity . . . ," Twitter, January 30, 2022, 11:03 p.m., https:// twitter.com/aliciatcrosby/status/1487999991369064453.

12. Danya Ruttenberg, "Institutional Obligations," in *On Repentance and Repair: Making Amends in an Unapologetic World* (Boston: Beacon, 2022), 109.

Chapter 9 Protecting the Land as Resistance

1. Mary Annaïse Heglar (@MaryHeglar), "'Humans' caused climate change . . . ," Twitter, August 10, 2021, 5:00 p.m., https://twitter.com/Mary Heglar/status/1425200403986239492.

2. Karen L. Smith-Janssen, "A Translator for the Climate Crisis, Grief Included," NRDC, May 4, 2020, https://www.nrdc.org/stories/translator-climate -crisis-grief-included.

3. Sarah Augustine, *The Land Is Not Empty: Following Jesus in Dismantling the Doctrine of Discovery* (Harrisonburg, VA: Herald, 2021), 27.

4. Vandana Shiva, *Reclaiming the Commons: Biodiversity, Indigenous Knowledge, and the Rights of Mother Earth* (Santa Fe, NM: Synergetic Press, 2020), 19.

5. Wangari Maathai, "Prof Wangari Maathai's Keynote Address during the 2nd World Congress of Agroforestry" (speech, World Congress of Agroforestry, Nairobi, Kenya, August 24, 2009), Green Belt Movement, https://www.green beltmovement.org/wangari-maathai/key-speeches-and-articles/2nd-world -congress-of-agroforestry-keynote-address.

6. Ayana Elizabeth Johnson and Katharine K. Wilkinson, eds., *All We Can Save: Truth, Courage, and Solutions for the Climate Crisis* (New York: One World, 2020), xviii.

7. Tara Houska, "Sacred Resistance," in Johnson and Wilkinson, *All We Can Save*, 216.

8. Houska, "Sacred Resistance," 218.

9. Mirabai Starr, epigraph to chap. 2, "Laying Down Our Burden," in *Wild Mercy* (Boulder, CO: Sounds True, 2019). Used by permission.

Chapter 10 Kinship as Resistance

1. Steven Charleston, *Ladder to the Light: An Indigenous Elder's Meditations on Hope and Courage* (Minneapolis: Broadleaf Books, 2021), 137.

2. Patty Krawec, *Becoming Kin: An Indigenous Call to Unforgetting the Past and Reimagining Our Future* (Minneapolis: Broadleaf Books, 2022), 19.

3. Brené Brown, *Braving the Wilderness: The Quest for True Belonging and the Courage to Stand Alone* (New York: Random House, 2017), 37.

Chapter 11 Decolonizing as Resistance

1. adrienne maree brown, *Pleasure Activism: The Politics of Feeling Good* (Chico, CA: AK Press, 2019), 10.

2. Kaitlin B. Curtice, *Native: Identity, Belonging, and Rediscovering God* (Grand Rapids: Brazos, 2020), 177.

3. Ian Cull et al., *Pulling Together: A Guide for Front-Line Staff, Student Services, and Advisors* (Victoria, BC: BCcampus, 2018), 7, https://opentext bc.ca/indigenizationfrontlineworkers/.

4. Billy Perrigo, "India's Farmers Are Leading One of the Largest Protests Yet against Modi's Government," *Time*, December 8, 2020, https://time.com /5918967/india-farmer-protests/.

5. Simran Jeet Singh, "The Farmers' Protests Are a Turning Point for India's Democracy," *Time*, February 11, 2021, https://time.com/5938041/india-farm er-protests-democracy/.

6. "A Brief Definition of Decolonization and Indigenization," Indigenous Corporate Training, Inc., March 29, 2017, https://www.ictinc.ca/blog/a-brief -definition-of-decolonization-and-indigenization.

7. "The True, Dark History of Thanksgiving," Citizen Potawatomi Nation, November 25, 2020, https://www.potawatomi.org/blog/2020/11/25/the -true-dark-history-of-thanksgiving/.

Chapter 12 Generosity as Resistance

1. "Potlatch," Living Tradition, last accessed June 20, 2022, https://umista potlatch.ca/potlatch-eng.php.

2. Gareth Higgins, *How Not to Be Afraid* (Minneapolis: Broadleaf, 2022), 4.

3. Kyle T. Mays, *An Afro-Indigenous History of the United States* (Boston: Beacon, 2021), xvi.

Chapter 13 Intergenerational Healing as Resistance

1. Clarissa Pinkola Estés, "Do Not Lose Heart. We Were Made for These Times," Findhorn New Story Hub, February 3, 2020, http://newstoryhub.com /2020/02/do-not-lose-heart-we-were-made-for-these-times-clarissa-pinkola -estes-ph-d-2/ .

2. Fergus Walker, "Inter-generational Resilience," The Alliance for Inter-generational Resilience, accessed February 13, 2022, https://intergenresil.com /resil-stories/fergus-cgf.html.

3. Louise Zimanyi, Helena Keeshig, and Lynn Short, "Children Make Connections to Aki (Earth) through Anishinaabe Teachings," The Conversation, April 19, 2020, https://theconversation.com/children-make-connections-to -aki-earth-through-anishinaabe-teachings-133669.

4. Iain MacKinnon, Lewis Williams, and Arianna Waller, "The Re-indigenization of Humanity to Mother Earth: A Learning Platform to Cultivate Social-Ecological Resilience and Challenge the Anthropocene," *Journal of Sustainability Education* 16 (2017), http://www.susted.com/wordpress/content /the-re-indigenization-of-humanity-to-mother-earth-a-learning-platform-to -cultivate-social-ecological-resilience-and-challenge-the-anthropocene_2018 _01/.

5. Tanya Tarr, "How to Better Stick to 2022 New Year's Resolutions, according to Behavioral Science," *Forbes*, January 2, 2022, https://www.forbes.com/sites/tanyatarr/2022/01/02/how-to-better-stick-to-2022-new-years-resolutions-according-to-behavioral-science/.

6. "Mission," Soul Fire Farm, last accessed June 15, 2022, https://www.soulfirefarm.org.

Chapter 14 Liminality as Resistance

1. Jenan Matari, "Embracing Your Identities," TEDx Talk, 6:08, filmed July 25, 2017 in Asbury Park, NJ, https://youtu.be/uYqVn-m__8Y.

2. Terry Tempest Williams, "Living in a Woman's Body: Like Earth, We Are Changing Quickly through the Violence of Climate Collapse," *The Guardian*, February 15, 2022, https://tinyurl.com/2p8fp3na.

Chapter 15 Facing History as Resistance

1. Angela Davis, *Freedom Is a Constant Struggle: Ferguson, Palestine, and the Foundations of a Movement* (Chicago: Haymarket Books, 2016), 1.

2. Joy Henderson, "While Canada Cracks Down on Indigenous and Black Protesters, White Supremacists Get a Free Pass in Canada," *Toronto Star*, January 29, 2022, https://tinyurl.com/eztaw8bz.

3. Stella Nyanzi, interview by Lizzy Davies, "'I'm Free at Last': Uganda's Rudest Poet Stella Nyanzi on Prison, Protest and Finding a New Voice in Germany," January 27, 2022, *The Guardian* (UK), https://www.theguardian.com/global-development/2022/jan/27/im-free-at-last-ugandas-rudest-poet-stella-nyanzi-on-prison-protest-and-finding-new-voice-in-germany.

Chapter 16 Integration as Resistance

1. Elaine Alec, *Calling My Spirit Back* (Victoria, BC: TellWell, 2020), 172.

2. Rabbi Alan Lew, *This Is Real and You Are Completely Unprepared: The Days of Awe as a Journey of Transformation* (New York: Little, Brown, 2003), 9.

3. Matt Haig, *The Midnight Library* (New York: Viking, 2020), 134.

Chapter 17 Interspiritual Relationship as Resistance

1. Pádraig Ó Tuama, *In the Shelter: Finding a Home in the World* (Minneapolis: Broadleaf Books, 2015), 53.

2. Valarie Kaur, *See No Stranger: A Memoir and Manifesto of Revolutionary Love* (New York: One World, 2021), 185.

3. Juliet Diaz, *The Altar Within: A Radical Devotional Guide to Liberate the Divine Self* (Trenton, NJ: Row House, 2022), xxvi.

Chapter 18 Prayer as Resistance

1. *Merriam-Webster*, s.v. "prayer," https://www.merriam-webster.com/diction ary/prayer.

2. Kaitlin Curtice, "The Lantern and the Wildflower," in *A Rhythm of Prayer: A Collection of Meditations for Renewal*, ed. Sarah Bessey (New York: Convergent Books, 2021), 107.

3. Mihee Kim-Kort, *Outside the Lines: How Embracing Queerness Will Transform Your Faith* (Minneapolis: Fortress, 2018), 23.

4. Danya Ruttenberg, *Nurture the Wow: Finding Spirituality in the Frustration, Boredom, Tears, Poop, Desperation, Wonder, and Radical Amazement of Parenting* (New York: Flatiron Books, 2016), 73.

5. Kaitlin B. Curtice, *Native: Identity, Belonging, and Rediscovering God* (Grand Rapids: Brazos, 2020), 63.

Chapter 19 Dreaming as Resistance

1. Arundhati Roy, "The Pandemic Is a Portal," *Financial Times*, April 3, 2020, https://www.ft.com/content/10d8f5e8-74eb-11ea-95fe-fcd274e920ca.

2. Cole Arthur Riley, *This Here Flesh: Spirituality, Liberation, and the Stories That Make Us* (New York: Convergent Books, 2022), 12.

Chapter 20 Lifelong Resistance

1. Kirsten Powers, *Saving Grace: Speak Your Truth, Stay Centered, and Learn to Coexist with People Who Drive You Nuts* (New York: Convergent Books, 2021), 14.

2. Rabbi Alan Lew, *This Is Real and You Are Completely Unprepared: The Days of Awe as a Journey of Transformation* (New York: Little, Brown, 2003), 59.

3. Tarana Burke, *Unbound: My Story of Liberation and the Birth of the Me Too Movement* (New York: Flatiron Books, 2021), 11.

4. adrienne maree brown, *Pleasure Activism: The Politics of Feeling Good* (Chico, CA: AK Press, 2019), 32.

5. Eric Holthaus, *The Future Earth: A Radical Vision for What's Possible in the Age of Warming* (New York: HarperOne, 2020), 50.

AUTHOR BIO

Kaitlin B. Curtice is an award-winning author, poet-storyteller, and public speaker. As an enrolled citizen of the Potawatomi nation, she writes on the intersections of spirituality and identity and how that shifts throughout our lives. She also speaks on these topics to diverse audiences who are interested in truth-telling and healing. As an interspiritual advocate, Kaitlin participates in conversations on topics such as colonialism in faith communities, and she has spoken at many conferences on the importance of interfaith relationships. She also writes online for *Sojourners*, Religion News Service, Apartment Therapy, *On Being, SELF Magazine*, and more. Her work has been featured on CBS and in *USA Today*. She also writes at *The Liminality Journal*. Kaitlin lives in Philadelphia with her family.